A Privateer's Voyage Round the World

A PRIVATEER'S VOYAGE ROUND THE WORLD

George Shelvocke

Edited with an introduction by
Vincent McInerney

Seaforth
PUBLISHING

This edition copyright © Vincent McInerney 2010

First published in Great Britain in 2010 by
Seaforth Publishing,
Pen & Sword Books Ltd,
47 Church Street,
Barnsley S70 2AS

www.seaforthpublishing.com

British Library Cataloguing in Publication Data

A catalogue record for this book is available
from the British Library

ISBN 978 1 84832 066 6

Typeset and designed by M.A.T.S. Leigh-on-Sea, Essex
Printed and bound in Great Britain by Cromwell Press Group

Contents

Contents

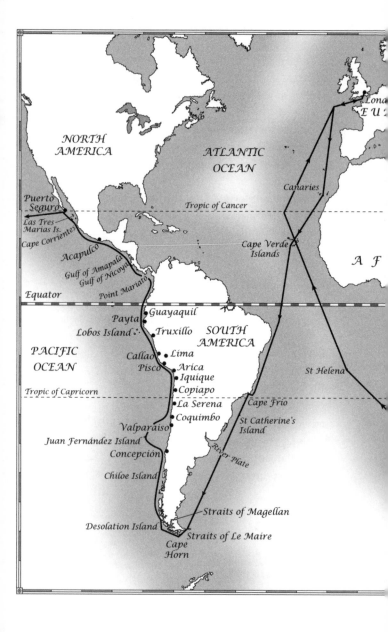

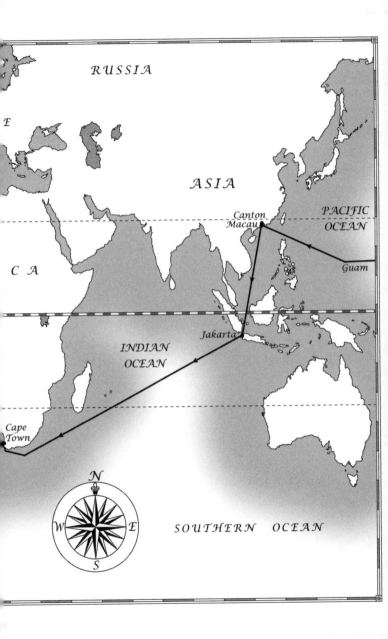

Editorial Note

The editions used for the main text are George
Shelvocke's *A Voyage Round the World by the way of
the Great South Sea, performed in the years 1719-1722*
(London: J. Senex, 1726); the Cassell Seafarers'
Library reprint with the invaluable introduction by
Perrin: Shelvocke, George, *A Voyage Round the World,*
with introduction and notes by W. G. Perrin (London:
Cassell, 1928); and the version given in Kerr's col-
lection of travels and voyages of 1894: Shelvocke,
George, *A Voyage Round the World in 1719-22* in
Robert Kerr's *A General History of Voyages and
Travels, Vols X & XI* (Edinburgh: Blackwood and
London: Cadell, 1824). The first edition of Betagh,
William, *A Voyage Round the World* (London:
Combes, Lacy, Clarke, 1728) was used.

The work has been reduced from about 90,000 words
to 40,000. Losses have been in the lengthy descriptions
of native peoples, flora and fauna. This may have been
an attempt by Shelvocke to be seen as a scientific
observer rather than a privateer, especially as 'the
author followed the custom of his age in . . . too often

plagiarising from earlier adventurers'.[1] Some aspects of the sea passages have also been edited. Spelling and punctuation and paragraphing have been adjusted to meet current expectations.

Introduction

> To investigate seafaring and colonial life is to find
> oneself in a world of hard men . . . never slow to take
> the shortest way with other men whose presence
> might mean danger.[2]

IN SPITE OF ITS sedate title, *A Privateer's Voyage Round
the World* written by George Shelvocke is an exciting
tale full of adventure and privateering in the Great
South Sea. First published in 1726, Shelvocke's work
was most probably written in a spirit of self-justification
and as an attempted defence against accusations of
piracy, and although the title would seem to hint more
at journeys of education and exploration made by a
gentleman traveller, this seaman's yarn encompasses
both the shipwrecks and sinkings of his buccaneering
exploits, as well as providing sensitive and vivid
accounts of the peoples and places he encountered on
his travels. As the second book in the series of Seafarers'
Voices, we once more find a seagoing voice from the
past taking us back to a time of danger and adventure,
in this case one where the protagonist treads a fine line
between the legality of privateering and the criminality

of the pirate. As with the first book in the series, Jean Marteilhe's *Galley Slave*, it seems that the author was keen to persuade the reader of the justice of his cause, and both accounts show us a barbarous world, although perhaps the barbarity was a little more explicit in Marteilhe's account of religious persecution. In Shelvocke's self-defence against any imputations of illegality, the sufferings of those on whom he preys are elided in the presentation of himself as a gentleman adventurer, albeit in a world where there is a strong sense of lawlessness, and authority is predicated on firepower.

George Shelvocke (*c*.1675-1742) took on the privateering command we read about in the following account in his mid-forties, after a career in the Royal Navy beginning in 1690. In 1703 he was appointed master of the thirty-two gun vessel, *Scarborough*, and in April 1704 Robert Harland, commander at Portsmouth, gave Shelvocke an acting commission as lieutenant which was confirmed by the Admiralty in November 1705. In December of that year Harland appointed his clerk, Edward Hughes, to the post of purser in the *Scarborough*, and Shelvocke and Hughes became shipmates, this being a connection Shelvocke would make use of when he fell on hard times later in life. Then in January 1706 Shelvocke was made third lieutenant of the ninety-gun *Association*, and he then moved to the *Britannia*, from which, in October 1706, he was paid off at Chatham as second lieutenant.

Unable to obtain another appointment at this rank, Shelvocke in July 1707 was appointed purser of the *Monck*, the previous holder of the post having been granted 'leave to resign' because of the ill-health of both body and accounts – it is unclear which indisposition came first. Shelvocke's new position was less prestigious that that of lieutenant, but far more lucrative, most pursers being reputed to possess the great alchemical gift of being able to turn seawater into gold; however, it seems that Shelvocke was unable to make his fortune in this post. His wife died in 1711 while he was still on the *Monck*, leaving him with a son, George Shelvocke the Younger, who later accompanied him on his privateering voyage around the world. In 1713 peace was declared with France, and Shelvocke was dismissed from the service and fell into poverty and want, lacking the 'interest' or connections necessary to procure him a pension or other suitable naval employment. As Hoffmann wrote, 'If they would take my advice, parents would never send a boy into the service without 'interest' . . . If they do, their child, if he behaves, may die possibly as a lieutenant, with scarcely an income to support himself; and should he be married with children, God help him, for no one else will!'[3]

In 1718, desperate, Shelvocke applied for help to his old shipmate, Edward Hughes, now a gentleman of property, and the principal shareholder in a consortium of merchants, the 'Gentleman-Adventurers', which was fitting-out two privateers to 'cruize', or prey, upon Spanish treasure ships in the Great South Sea, as the Pacific Ocean was then known. Privateers were privately-owned armed merchantmen acting under an official commission from the state, validated by a document allowing them to attack and plunder vessels belonging to enemies with whom that state was at war, the document being known as a 'letter of marque'.

The authorisation bestowed by the letter of marque put a vessel and its crew on official war-footing. The first letter of marque on record was issued by Henry III in February 1243 to one George Pyper, and privateers then operated until the signing of the Declaration of Paris in 1856 when the practice was officially discontinued. Over the centuries that privateers operated, the crew of a prize ship would be made prisoner and its cargo confiscated. If geographically feasible, the capture would be sailed to a friendly port, often containing an admiralty court. At this court the vessel would be 'condemned', or assessed at a price, and auctioned to produce prize money. If taken in enemy waters, the prize might be ransomed back to its captain, or to its owners, any monies from the ransom or sale of a prize being divided among those groups with a financial interest in the privateer.

This financial interest in the profits of privateering was generally divided between the venture capitalists who owned and fitted out the vessel, the crew of the privateer, and finally the crown or government of the country to which the privateer belonged. The entrepreneurs and the crew generally divided ninety per cent of the profits on a basis previously agreed, usually in a ratio of two to one. The final ten per cent would be due to the state which provided the letter of marque. In effect, privateers were a way of producing fighting ships and crews without the state having to spend public money, or commissioning naval officers. Privateers played a further role in forcing an enemy to use warships to convoy their own merchantmen, so tying themselves up as birds of passage rather than birds of prey. Privateers and their crews, it might be argued, represented a lesser form of total war, their object in any confrontation being to capture an enemy vessel with as little damage as possible, rather than to destroy it completely, the more complete the prize and its cargo being, the greater the potential profit.

Crews of privateers tended to be much larger than those of non-combative merchant ships, sometimes even outnumbering those of naval vessels, as the ability to furnish enough men to control a prize was crucial. Once an enemy merchantman was taken, a crew from the privateer had to be put on board to guard the crew of the prize, and to deliver the prize ship back to the appropriate port. There were cases where a privateer would take two, three, or more ships, all of which then had to be manned by personnel from the privateer, and this meant a large complement was necessary. We see this in Shelvocke's account, when he leaves too few of his crewmen on a prize ship together with their Spanish prisoners whilst he sails off to pursue another ship, only to return to find his men overpowered and murdered.

There were two ships funded by Hughes' consortium: the *Success*, a vessel of 350 tons, with a complement of thirty-six guns and 180 men, and the *Speedwell* – 200 tons, twenty-two guns, and 106 men. After a meeting with Hughes, Shelvocke emerged with a twenty-pound loan, having been given the captaincy of the *Success*, and made commander-in-chief of the expedition. The captain of the second ship, the *Speedwell*, would be John Clipperton, who had sailed with William Dampier (1651-1715) on Dampier's famous privateering expedition in 1703-04 to the Pacific Ocean – Clipperton was thus familiar with that part of the world to which they were headed.

Unfortunately for Shelvocke and his backers, England was not at this moment at war with Spain, although the expectation was that war was imminent. In the event, it was decided to take a shortcut that could be made available within the world of the letters of marque: 'it was possible to obtain a licence from a foreign sovereign to attack and rob *his* enemies.'[4] The foreign sovereign in this case was Charles VI of Austria, who was already at war with Spain. In November 1718, Shelvocke was sent to Ostend, then under Charles VI's control, to acquire this commission, hire some Flemish seamen, and stock up on 'liquors' for the voyage. The document, stating that '[t]he said Captain Shelvocke may make use of the Imperial Commission in warring against the Spaniards', was successfully obtained.

It is at this point we encounter the first tensions inherent in Shelvocke's story. There is another account of Shelvocke's *Voyage Round the World* which provides an insistent counterpoint to his account of himself and his adventures: this version, written by his captain of marines, another former purser named William Betagh, was also entitled *Voyage Round the World*, which was published two years after Shelvocke's in 1728. Shelvocke and Betagh seem to have had a disagreement of some sort at the beginning of the venture which is never explained fully in either account, Shelvocke merely writing, in August/early September 1718 off the southeast coast of South America that Betagh apparently said 'he felt I was prepossessed in his disfavour for words he spoke to me seven or eight months agone.' Whatever this initial argument, it appears to have been enough to provoke a fierce enmity between the two, and the two men provide parallel but conflicting versions of events as they sail around the world and back, a web of assertion and counter-assertion which is impossible to untangle.

Betagh's account is critical of Shelvocke's conduct right from the beginning of the venture. According to him, when Shelvocke returned to the Downs during the first week in December 1718, Hughes and his co-investors found that Shelvocke had hired more Flemings than authorised, had flown imperial colours, 'made entertainments' and 'fir'd away five barrels of powder',[5] and broached the wines and spirits. Shelvocke was immediately demoted, and Clipperton appointed as expedition commander and given the flagship, the *Success*. Shelvocke was left with public humiliation, the *Speedwell*, and a smouldering violent resentment against Clipperton, whom as he saw as not having been trained in 'the only nursery for sea officers,' the Royal Navy.[6]

Then on 17 December 1718, war was formally declared between England and Spain, which meant that the Flemings and their letter of marque could be packed off back to Ostend, and an English letter of marque obtained: this happened on 1 January 1719, at a cost of £41 17s 4d. Originally it had been intended that the *Speedwell* and *Success* would leave in November 1718 to double Cape Horn, passing through the Straits of Magellan or the Straits of Le Maire by December 1718 or January 1719, the southern summer. Normally the exact choice of route would have been left to the individual captain depending on factors such as the weather, currents, or time of year, and in the owners' 'Scheme of the Voyage' they suggest the Straits of Magellan, but Shelvocke chose the Straits of Le Maire, blaming Clipperton for having appropriated all the charts, although, of course, it could also have been a deliberate ploy to separate himself from Clipperton's ship. But due to the various delays, it was not until 13 February 1719 that the two ships finally set sail, with Shelvocke and Clipperton and their officers and marines all clad in scarlet suits provided by the Hughes syndicate.

Betagh was part of the crew until he was taken prisoner by the Spanish in February 1721 in a skirmish off the coast of Peru. Betagh claims that even prior to his capture, on the voyage out, he had come to the conclusion that Shelvocke was guilty of fraud upon the Hughes syndicate and also responsible for 'many other abuses and forgeries'.[7] Whilst a prisoner of the Spanish, Betagh wrote to Hughes of his suspicions about Shelvocke, and on his return to England in October 1721, in advance of Shelvocke, made further allegations. He claimed that Shelvocke had deliberately wrecked the *Speedwell* in the Juan Fernández Islands, in order to build a new vessel, the argument being that anything he took after this in the way of plunder would belong to him, Shelvocke, and not the owners of the original vessel. Clipperton arrived home in June 1722, only to die a few days afterwards apparently 'heart-broke . . . at his long run of misfortune'.[8] Shelvocke, the last of the trio, finally reached London on 1 August 1722 and Hughes, on Betagh's assertions, immediately had Shelvocke confined to the Wood Street Compter. Hughes attempted to have Shelvocke tried for piracy, but insufficient evidence was found. Common law was then invoked, unsuccessfully, but an appeal to the Court of Chancery saw a writ issued against Shelvocke. When it came to be served, it was found that Shelvocke had mysteriously escaped from prison. Then came a further accusation of piracy from the Spanish ambassador, and at this point Shelvocke vanished from sight for a time.

Shelvocke resurfaced in 1724-25 to present a hand-written account of his voyage to the Admiralty, written, no doubt, in part as a defence and justification to counter Betagh's verbal accusations, but also possibly with an eye to making money out of his tale of adventure on the high seas, as had several previous voyagers operating in a similar field. William Dampier had combined a life of exploration and privateering, and his very popular *New Voyage Round the World* (1697) had been followed by two volumes of *A Voyage to New Holland* in 1703 and 1709. In 1712 Woodes Rogers had published *A Cruising Voyage Round the World*, an account which had accompanied Shelvocke on his own voyage. Even more recently Daniel Defoe's *Robinson Crusoe*, a novel set around and about the places Shelvocke had visited, and inspired by the tale of Alexander Selkirk, another privateer, whom Rogers and Dampier had found marooned on one of the isles of Juan Fernández, had been published in 1719, the year of Shelvocke's departure, and had been a runaway success. Shelvocke's account, *A Voyage round the World by Way of the Great South Sea, Perform'd in the Years 1719, 20,*

21, 22 was published in 1726. Not only is this a detailed account of his privateering exploits, he also includes methodical descriptions of the flora and fauna of the places he visits, and descriptions of the inhabitants of some of the islands he visits, almost anthropological in their detail, as if he is self-consciously playing down the buccaneering aspects of his voyage by elevating himself to role of scientific observer, and placing himself firmly in the pantheon of adventuring explorers in the mode of Dampier and Rogers.

Betagh, seeing himself maligned in Shelvocke's book, published his version of the voyage in 1728. As Perrin says, Shelvocke is: 'certainly a readable and entertaining author.'[9] Betagh is perhaps equally so when he allows style and humour to predominate over his apparent tendency to anger and speculation.

Shelvocke's account, when added to that of Betagh, takes us into the world of what Sabin identifies as 'about the last of the buccaneering voyages'[10] that had begun in Elizabethan times with the voyages of Drake and Raleigh. In the company of Shelvocke we embark for three years in a small wooden sailing craft where time is measured by half-hour sandglasses being turned and ever re-turned, there being no chronometers, and where longitude is uncertain; where supplies and water are critical and must be replenished at short intervals, meaning incessant labour working the ship in and out of badly charted, or completely uncharted, ports. This is a world where new diseases may arrive on board daily, and the old ones refuse to leave, and the only constants are lice, vermin, lack of sanitary facilities, extreme heat and cold, lack of privacy, and extreme overcrowding. Life on board these vessels seems to have been characterised by continual drunkenness when liquor was available and, perhaps inevitably given the circumstances, constant arguments, fights and mutinies. These ships were places where death by the gun, or drowning, or disease, threatened daily.

Before we enter into that world perhaps there is something to say about the nature of privateers in general. To help instruct in the speediest and most thorough ways of disabling an enemy, privateering advice manuals became very popular in the eighteenth century. Directed at both professionals and hopeful amateurs, they were full of hints regarding the various types of attack that would return best results. Hutchinson, writing in the late eighteenth century states that '[t]he most sure and likely method to make an easy conquest . . . is to run close up across her stern firing and raking fore and aft . . . that if the shots miss the rudder, etc., . . . they may do the greatest execution possible so as to distress them to make a submission.'[11] In other words, as we see from Shelvocke's account, the legalised piracy of privateering was most definitely predicated on terrifying likely victims into submission. There is no doubt that successful privateering could pay significant dividends: as the French admiral, Villeneuve, wrote: 'On board the *Bucentaure*, off the Azores, the 4th Messidor. My Lord, – I have the honour to inform your Excellency, that yesterday morning the advanced frigates discerned two sail . . . coming from Lima with a very rich cargo. . . . estimated from five to six millions.'[12] The fortunes of whole ports were seen as being connected with the prowess of their privateers, as evidenced by a Liverpool Memorandum Book published in 1753, which states that '[i]n the last war, 1739 to 1748, trade flourished so extensively that, pursued it seven years longer, it would have enlarged the size and riches of the town to a prodigious degree.'[13] The privateersmen themselves seem to have been feted on account of their reputed daring and reckless courage, and the potential for profit no doubt made such an occupation much more attractive than being forcibly recruited into the navy. An 'Old Stager' writes that:

[a]s men were safe by *Letter of Marque* from impressment, the most daring and dashing sailors came out of their hiding holes. On the day when the vessel left dock, the captain or owner generally gave a grand dinner and she cruised the river with music playing . . . colours flying . . . as she dashed like a flying fish through the waters. And the crew! The Captain, some daring man who had fought his way to the position. His officers elected for the same quality . . . While the men! What a reckless, dreadnought,

dare-devil collection of human beings . . . ready to
obey every order, the more desperate, the better.'[14]

However, it was also in the interests of these buccaneering adventurers to cultivate a reputation of
ruthlessness and maintain a ferocious image in order to
persuade potential victims to surrender rather than
resist. The literature of piracy and privateering is full
of possibly apocryphal tales which no doubt added to
the fearsomeness of their reputation. Apparently,
Richard Grenville (1542-1591) was inclined to demon-
strate to the Spanish some attributes of the archetypal
privateersman by crushing wine glasses between his
teeth (naturally after emptying them) 'and swallowing
them down, so that blood ran out of his mouth'[15] whilst
in the case of Henry Morgan (1635-1688) he might be
seen applying some judicious torture, or using priests
as human shields: it seems that he 'compelled priests
and nuns from nearby convents to carry these ladders
to the walls under the murderous fire of the defen-
ders.'[16] If it were Edward 'Blackbeard' Teach (d.1718),
it was said of his appearance that he would be 'hidden
behind a greasy mass of black hair falling halfway to
his waist . . . his clothes filthy with spilt drink and blood
. . . his body stinking of sweat and the rum and
gunpowder that was his customary drink. . . . With
lighted matches under his hat appearing on each side of
his face . . . a Fury from Hell could not look more

frightful.'[17] The importance of public image and
reputation seems to have been quite clear to these
adventurers, and must also have been a factor in the
strength of their leadership and ability to maintain the
loyalty and obedience of a potentially recalcitrant or
mutinous crew. Shelvocke complains of disloyalty and
insubordination in his account, and gives us a tale of
mutiny and faction fighting. In his eagerness to present
himself as much-maligned, but honourable and fair in
his dealings with others, we glimpse an ideal of a
gentleman-explorer, sensitive to the cultures and places
which he encounters, which sits uneasily with the
reality of the privateering life where the difference
between the privateer and pirate is no wider than the
letter of marque.

The accounts of both Shelvocke and Betagh together
give a unique insight into the world of the privateer, but
as each calls the integrity of the other into question, the
reader must be left to decide which writer is more
convincing. As Spate puts it: '[t]he pair (Betagh and
Shelvocke) were obviously hard liars both; though it
would be as difficult as impossible to decide which was
the more atrocious traducer.'[18] A privateering adventure
of the type on which Shelvocke, Clipperton and Betagh
had embarked had much potential for profit, but we
have also seen that such a venture was a risky affair,
and that a fine line divided the legally authorised
privateer from the pirate as criminal. All of the

participants must have been aware of the horrible example of Captain Kidd before them, who had begun a voyage as a privateer, a voyage which had ended with his being convicted and hanged as a pirate, in a case which still inspires disputes about his guilt and innocence today. Hence we find in the text Shelvocke's eagerness to emphasise the rights and wrongs of his own case in the face of the allegations against him.

While preparing for the voyage, both captains had been given a copy of Woodes Rogers *A Cruising Voyage Round The World* (1712), which included a good description of the island of Juan Fernández, one of the rendezvous points should their vessels *Speedwell* and *Success* become separated. From Rogers' book Shelvocke would have learned that life was relatively easily supported on Juan Fernández, and that there were plenty of trees to supply wood, should a sizeable amount of wood be needed for any reason – to construct a ship, perhaps, and we have seen that Betagh asserts that Shelvocke had this intention in mind. Six days after sailing Clipperton and Shelvocke became separated – again, whether this was intentional on either part is under dispute by the participants – but in spite of prearranged rendezvous points, the vessels continued their journeys separately, Clipperton, according to Perrin, 'reluctantly, for not only was his prospect of success lessened . . . but also the whole stock of wines and spirits was on board the *Speedwell*, and the prospect of facing a passage through the Straits of Magellan in a temperance ship was not pleasing.'[19]

Alcohol plays a major part in these buccaneering adventures: it buys compromises and friendships, it fuels mutinies, and the lack of it on the *Success* is blamed for the deaths of some of Clipperton's crew through disease and exposure, at a time when various forms of alcohol were considered important medicinally. Drink is used to explain an accusation against Clipperton of cowardice in the face of the enemy, a terrible charge, and the nature of Betagh's vitriolic attitude towards Shelvocke is evident in his claim that Shelvocke used up the combined liquor for two ships for three years in the first twelve months of the voyage through his personal consumption of 'hippsy, a liquor compounded of wine, water and brandy, which by the admirers of it, is also called meat, drink and cloth.'[20]

Betagh in his account is also quick to criticise Shelvocke's son, George Shelvocke the Younger, as someone who:

> . . . knew nothing of sea affairs, nor anything else commendable or manly. His employment at London was to dangle after women, and gossip at the tea-table. Aboard us . . . to overhear all that was said, then tell his father . . . Yet this insignificant fellow had £660 prize money, in prejudice to many honest brave men, destroy'd, lost and beggar'd at their captain's pleasure.'[21]

He also questions Shelvocke's judgement in replacing his chief mate, Pedder, with his cabin steward, Matthew Stewart, saying that although Stewart was 'a young man of good sense and good education', he was 'not seaman enough to distinguish between a brace and a bowline',[22] and Perrin's opinion is that it was an 'extraordinary advancement.'[23]

Shelvocke's first privateering move vividly demonstrates the way in which it was possible to profit from popular fears about buccaneering and the reputation of pirates for violence, without actually having to resort to violence. The *Speedwell* encountered a Portuguese merchantman at Cape Frio, and Shelvocke immediately hoisted his imperial colours from Ostend, a black double eagle on yellow ground. Betagh comments that 'pyrates have a yellow field and black human skeleton; which at a small distance are not easily distinguished, especially in light gales of wind.'[24] In other words, any ship flying such a flag could be mistaken for a pirate, and the captain of the Portuguese vessel certainly fell into such an error. When Shelvocke's 'second captain',[25] Hately, is sent aboard ostensibly to 'buy tobacco' he receives a number of valuable 'presents', plus extracting a purse of three hundred gold moidores[26] from the captain. Betagh gives as a further reason for the quick surrender of his gold by the Portuguese captain the fear of having to undergo:

> . . . that piece of discipline used by the merry blades
> in the West-Indies, call'd 'Blooding and Sweating';
> which is done by making the captain, on declining to
> discover his money, to run the gauntlet naked thro'
> the pyrate's crew; each of them furnish'd with a sail-
> needle, pricking him in the buttocks, back and
> shoulders. And thus bleeding, they put him into a
> sugar cask swarming with cockroaches, cover him
> with a blanket, and there leave him to glut the vermin
> with his blood.'[27]

Reading of the easy capitulation of this ship and the
disinclination of other vessels to engage with Shelvocke
and his meagre forces, it should be remembered what
was involved in a privateer boarding skirmish:

> One cannot imagine the horrors of half-an-hour's
> fight on a boarded ship, where six or seven hundred
> men find themselves pressed into a space some 120
> feet long and 30 feet wide, exchanging blows with
> axes and cutlasses, being run through by thrusts of
> pikes, pierced by bullets and shattered by exploding
> grenades. Amidst the thunder of cannon fire, and the
> shrieks of the dying, it is a scene impossible to
> describe.'[28]

It is unsurprising that so often the privateers met with
so little resistance.

Whilst Shelvocke then presents himself as a hapless
and helpless victim of circumstances, with little choice
of action in the face of a factious and mutinous crew,

Betagh pictures the events as being manipulated by Shelvocke with the aim of furthering the personal and family interests of the latter. At this distance in time and space the rights and wrongs of the issue are almost impossible to untangle, but whatever the justice of the situation, Shelvocke produces a narrative which vividly evokes the uncertainties and dangers inherent in the life of the privateer captain on an expedition where the risks and dangers are commensurate with the potential rewards. It is difficult now to identify with those who led such lives, yet Shelvocke's talents for description effortlessly transport us back to the ships and uncharted waters of his day.

One of the most interesting and ironic characteristics of Shelvocke's account of his voyage is the way that he is unknowingly skirting the edges of history, and in this way the tale is full of retrospective significance for the modern reader. One such event is the incident that was to give Simon Hately, Shelvocke's second captain, lasting peripheral literary fame, though none would have been more surprised than he at these posthumous laurels. For several days the ship had been followed by a 'solitary black albatross.' Hately, thinking this 'might be of some ill omen . . . at length shot the albatross not doubting we should have a fair wind after that.' Almost eighty years later, in 1797, the poets Samuel Taylor Coleridge and William Wordsworth were discussing ideas for the poem *The Rime of the Ancient Mariner* which Coleridge was in the process of writing, and Wordsworth, who had been reading Shelvocke's account of his voyage, suggested the albatross incident as a suitable motif. Coleridge accepted the suggestion, and Simon Hately's killing of the albatross entered literary history.

Another little skirmish with history occurs when Shelvocke takes a ship, the *Rosario*, carrying guano and dismisses the cargo as 'useless' to him, although he acknowledges its worth locally. It was to be a hundred years before guano was to reach Europe in quantity and in the process effect a transformation in agriculture. Again, in California Shelvocke seems to have discovered gold when he writes that 'the soil . . . appears as if intermingled with gold-dust. We endeavoured to wash and purify some of this, and the more this was done, the more it appeared like gold.' Yet he loses his soil samples in China and the Californian gold rush must wait another hundred years or so.

Shelvocke also gives us an account of the Indians he meets, one unlike all the others in the book in its complimentary tone regarding the people and their way of life. His description of the indigenous tribes of California incorporates the concept of the noble savage, and he describes the manner in which American Indians share food and live peaceably, presenting them in stark contrast to the way in which he pictures his own crew with their disputes over authority and shares of the spoils, while again implicitly separating himself from such petty squabbles in an assertion of anthropological superiority.

Shelvocke's narrative ability to distance himself from the reality of the privateering project, and efface its affinity with piracy, is also evident in his account of his adventures in China where he complains of being 'on the brink of falling into the bottomless pit of Chinese avarice.' Ironically, he is critical of the mode of operation of the East India Company in China, and what he sees as their unjust appropriation of his funds, though he has been happily 'taxing' others in a similar way throughout his narrative. His ability to evade acknowledgement of the implications of his actions also seems to have extended to avoiding the consequences of being accused of piracy, as we have seen.

It seems impossible at this distance to know exactly what occurred. According to Betagh, Shelvocke, after landing back in England in August 1722 tried to bribe Hughes by a 'genteel donation', only for Hughes to give Shelvocke in charge and have him 'carry'd to the Cockpit.' Hughes then took out an action against Shelvocke at Doctors' Commons, and another at common law, which led to his being confined in Wood Street Compter. After this, Hughes applied to the Admiralty for a warrant to keep Shelvocke in custody, in order for him to be tried for a piracy on the Portuguese, and for robberies on the King of Spain's subjects, as well as defrauding the owners – not dissimilar to the charges faced by Captain Kidd. The court refused Hughes a warrant, because no witness could be found to say that they had seen the three hundred moidores taken out of the Portuguese captain's escritoire, as was claimed. Hughes now tried the Court of Chancery, where the Lord Chancellor granted a writ against Shelvocke for £8,000, but the latter 'contrived so with the marshal of the King's Bench prison that he escaped on a Sunday; and prevented the said writ in chancery being served upon him; and has ever since absconded.'[29]

A writ of rebellion was now issued against Shelvocke, but his brother-in-law went to two of the owners (complainants also named in the bill) and made some sort of 'composition', or mutual agreement with them, so that the prosecution was halted. Betagh complained bitterly of a 'writ granted by the highest officer in the kingdom not being able to secure an offender, who has found means by corrupt practices to prevent the execution of it.' Betagh also complained that Shelvocke had imposed 'a scandalous narrative upon the world', dedicated to the Lords of the Admiralty in order to 'court them for favours, while there are repeated letters from the king of Spain to demand satisfaction for depredations upon his subjects, committed by this very man', although even Betagh admitted that 'now Great Britain and Spain are at such variance' it would be difficult to predict the outcome.[30]

By Betagh's account the final judgement on the question may be that Shelvocke survived to live and die in peace and plenty by a combination of circumstances: bribery, courting the Admiralty, the fact of England and Spain being at war, and by knowing how and where to lay low, and for how long; and, finally, as Betagh observes 'through the courts of justice either wanting the inclination or power to punish him.'[31]

But whatever the rights and wrongs of the case, in spite of Betagh's and Hughes' accusations, which could have had fatal consequences for him, Shelvocke lived on until 1742, dying at age 66 at the residence of his son, 'Georgy', in Lombard Street in the city of London. Georgy had become Secretary to the General Post Office, certainly an advancement on crewing a privateer, and he eventually became an FRS and an FSA, and produced, in 1757, his own version of his father's book – full of careful editing.[32] It seems that both father and son had a way with words.

In terms of what profits the Shelvockes, father and son, had made from privateering, the figures, as would be expected, are conflicting. According to Perrin, a few days after Shelvocke arrived back in England in August 1722, Matthew Stewart, the cabin steward turned chief mate, landed at Dover where he was seized, and a book found on him which gave the division of the booty. In this Shelvocke had received £2642 10s and Shelvocke's son, George, whose rank is described as 'Nothing', received £660.[33] Betagh claims this only represented the sale of the silver, without any mention of the gold that had been taken, and Betagh puts Shelvocke's eventual haul at something in the region of £25,000. Possibly the figure lies somewhere between the two. But the value of Shelvocke's legacy to the modern reader is incalculable. He has left us with an unforgettable account of the high seas, a gripping tale of adventure from beginning to end, and it is for the reader to decide whether to admire him for his integrity in the face of personal difficulty, as it seems that Shelvocke would have us do, or whether to admire him for an astonishing ability not only to survive the dangers of such a voyage, but also to live on and enjoy the profits of his adventures.

A Privateer's Voyage Round the World

Prologue: The Scheme of the Voyage

VOYAGE TO THE Great South Sea to cruise upon the
Spaniards under His Majesty's Commission with two
ships, viz.

The *Success* of 350 tons, 36 guns, 180 men, commanded by Capt. John Clipperton, and the *Speedwell* of
200 tons, 22 guns and 106 men commanded by Capt.
George Shelvocke. With eighteen months' provisions at
short allowance.

To make your passage you must get clear of the
English Channel in the middle of November, then you
have three months to get into the Straits of Magellan
(though you may get this passage in six weeks). In the
Straits you must wood, water, and clean your ships,
which brings on the end of January: the Southern
summer. So the beginning of February you will be in
the South Sea, the properest season of the year.

By the middle of March you'll get off Payta (lat. 5° S)
for in that month the King of Spain's ships sail from
Lima for Panama with the King's treasure: usually in
three ships from 20 to 36 guns. If you meet and take
them, your voyage and fortune will be made, and you
might return to Europe by going over between Australia

and New Guinea, touching at Mauritius before returning by way of the Cape of Good Hope.

Should you not get down early enough in March to meet the King's ships, you must cruise until you take enough small vessels to enable you to attack and take Guayaguil, Ecuador (lat. 2° 11' S). Should you take this place before they can remove their riches, you will undoubtedly have such as will be sufficient, as there is seldom less than three millions of dollars in the King's warehouse.

Should you be disappointed of this treasure, then proceed for Payta, northwest Peru (lat. 5° 5' S) and Collan, which two lie a small mile from each other. Both of these, about 350 miles from Guayaquil, may be taken at the same time, and should you take all three you will have no need to cruise upon the Acapulco treasure ship, but will make the best of your way to the Juan Fernández Islands (lat. 33° S 40° W) to wood and water, and then return to Europe the same way you came into those seas which will be about the month of January back again.

Should any accident prevent you taking those places, make the best of way to the coast of Mexico and clean your ships at Tres Marias Islands (lat. 21° 38' N) or the Gulf of Nicaragua (lat. 9° N) and after wooding, watering and victualling with turtle, proceed to Acapulco (lat. 16° 51' N) for the Acapulco treasure ship and lie there the month of December twenty-four miles

from land with the smaller ship, the *Speedwell*, nearer
the shore. And should you take this ship proceed to
Mauritius, and if you want water, stop at the island of
Guam (13° N 145° E).

If this fails wait at Tres Marias till the next February
and be off Acapulco 24 March, for the outward bound
Acapulco ship will sail that day. Suppose she escape
you, but you gain intelligence she has sailed, pursue her
to Guam where she always puts in for refreshment.
Should you miss her there make the best of your way to
the Mauritius.

Owners' (Gentlemen-Adventurers) Instructions

1. From England to the isle of St Catherine, Brazil. We leave Plymouth in company with our consort, the *Success*, Captain Clipperton, but are separated in a storm. I encounter the first of he mutinies against me. We fail to rendezvous with Captain Clipperton at the Canary Islands, and the Cape Verde Islands, and strike westward across the Atlantic for St Catherine's Island, Brazil.

SAILING FROM PLYMOUTH in the *Speedwell*, on 13 February 1719, in company with the *Success*, under Captain Clipperton, we separated six days later on the 19th when, between nine and ten at night, we encountered such a violent storm that on the *Speedwell* we had to take in all sail and run under bare poles. At midnight, we were struck by a sea that stove in a deadlight on our quarter, and another on our stern. Through these we shipped a vast quantity of water, and were in great apprehension of foundering before we could get them fastened up again.

By 20 February we could no longer see the *Success*, and this storm so terrified the greater part of my crew, that seventy of them wished to bear away back to England, alleging that the ship was so ill-found she would never carry us to the South Sea. I told them if the ship was unstable it was because we were overburdened aloft, but would eat and drink her into better trim. For, as we used our provisions in the hold, we could then send down the guns to steady her weight. But all I said was to little purpose, as they continued in their insolence to demand I clap the helm a-weather and steer for home, and I was obliged to arm my officers to bring the malcontents to reason. At this, the mutineers soon dispersed. I made two fast to the lower yard tackles, to receive, in time, their deserved punishment, but was then approached by the rest of the crew who came in a very submissive manner asking me to pardon the two malefactors.

I agreed, and, as all now seemed tractable, I ordered up some brandy, and we drank to our prosperous voyage, etc., and I found that the dram, once or twice repeated, proved the best means of oversetting their wicked intentions, and to bring them back to their duty.

All went quietly until 24 February when Simon Hately, my second captain, through an excess of indiscretion and self-conceit, now began disputing the command of the ship with me, telling me on deck in front of the ship's company that he had private orders from one of the chief of the Gentlemen-Adventurers, and Captain Clipperton, to take charge of the ship (I had reason to believe he spoke true as to the latter). I asked if he had a private commission, or letter of marque, to which he returned only an expression of contempt, saying that he should have the command by being the only person on the ship with knowledge of the South Seas. How far this might have prevailed amongst the people, the crew, who had already begun one mutiny themselves and were no doubt ripe for another, especially under so high-ranking an officer, I cannot say, had not his unseamanlike behaviour in the late storm rendered him ridiculous, an object of derision, and obviously unfit for command. Still, I was uneasy to find myself among a ship's crew from whom I could expect nothing but trouble and vexation, for it was reasonable to assume that those who could dare to be so insolent near home, when I might have in a day or two brought them to justice, would stick at nothing in some remote part where they might find some plausible pretence (however unreasonable) for continual disobedience.

The Canary Isles had been settled as the first place of rendezvous, should the ships be separated. We arrived there on 17 March 1719, only to learn later Captain Clipperton had already left on the 15th. We cruised there the time appointed by our instructions: ten days, during which nothing happened except I sent off the launch to make a prize of a small vessel we saw. Though she was hardly worth the trouble, containing only a small quantity of slate, and a quarter-cask of wine, the greater part of which the boat's crew drank before they brought her back to the *Speedwell*.

On 29 March we sailed, with our prize, for the Cape Verde Islands, the crew being so discontented I thought it best to stow the arms in the bread room. We arrived there on 4 April, again to find Captain Clipperton already departed.

A little before arriving at this island, Turner Stevens, the gunner, very gravely proposed that we cruise the Red Sea, saying there could be no harm in robbing the Mahometans, whereas the Spaniards were good Christians, whom it was a sin to injure. I ordered him immediately into confinement, after which he became outrageous, threatening to blow up the ship, wherefore I discharged him at his own request, and also left on shore my chief mate, Andrew Pedder, who had challenged and fought with Mr Brooks, my first lieutenant. In place of Pedder, as mate, I now put Mathew Stewart, my cabin steward.

After cruising until 18 April 1719, we went to Port Praya, in the island of St Jago, but finding nothing here but fair promises, I sold our prize for 150 dollars. Six men deserted here, and there being a Portuguese ship in the harbour I told the captain thereof to go ashore in search of my men, otherwise I would take six of his. By this means I recovered two of my own, who fell on their knees asking my pardon.

I now resolved to proceed to the isle of St Catherine on the coast of Brazil (lat. 20° 30' S) in hopes of obtaining every thing necessary for our passage into the South Sea, as, according to earlier authors, St Catherine abounds in all the necessities for long voyages. We sailed, therefore, from Port Praya on 20 April 1719, and had a very bad passage, taking twenty-one days to cross the Equator because of the most variable weather that can be conceived: slight breezes, varying all round the compass, and sometimes heavy squalls of wind, with thunder, lightning, and rain.

After fifty-five days, on 4 June 1719, we made Cape Frio (23° 41' S) on the coast of Brazil where on 5 June meeting a ship, I ordered the five-oar boat hoisted out and sent across with Captain Hately to enquire the news on the coast. I also gave him money to buy tobacco, as the *Success* had our stock on board (as well as other things) which had created a west country famine amongst us. When Hately returned he told me she was a Portuguese from Rio de Janeiro, bound to Pernambuco, and that he could get no tobacco, but had laid out my money in china cups and plates, nests of drawers, China silk, sweetmeats, bananas, plantains and pumpkins, etc. I gave him to understand I was not pleased with him squandering my money in such a manner, to which he answered he thought what he did was for the best, that he had laid out his own money as well as mine, and that, to his knowledge, the things he bought would sell for double at the next port. I assured him I did not like his proceedings by any means.

We weighed from Cape Frio; and on Friday, 19 June 1719, at eleven in the morning, we made the northernmost end of the island of St Catherine (lat. 27° S). St

Catherine is about twenty-five miles long, but nowhere exceeds six miles broad; in one place the channel between it and the mainland of South America is only a quarter of a mile wide. The island is covered all over with impassable woods, except where cleared for plantations. These plantations contain a great abundance of oranges, both China and Seville, lemons, citrons, limes, bananas, cabbage-palms, melons of all sorts, and potatoes. They also grow very large and good sugar canes, of which they make little use for want of utensils, so that the little sugar, molasses and rum they have is very dear. Sassafras, so much valued in Europe, is so common here that we laid in a good quantity for fuel. All else is dense wood, and even the nearby smaller island is covered in like manner with a great variety of trees, between which the ground is entirely covered with thorns and brambles, which hinder all access.

They have very little game, though the woods are full of parrots, which are good eating. These birds always fly in pairs, often several hundreds in a flock. Macaws, cockatoos, plovers, and a variety of other birds of curious colours and various shapes are to be seen in abundance, particularly one somewhat larger than a thrush, having a spur on the joint of each wing. Flamingos are also seen here in great numbers, of a fine scarlet colour, and appear very beautiful while flying. This bird is about the size of a heron, and like it in shape.

The fishery is here is also excellent – of all sorts and in great plenty, and to be easily taken by net. All the creeks and bays are well stocked with mullets, large rays, grantors, cavallies, and drum fish, so named from the noise they make when followed into shallow water. Some of them weigh twenty or thirty pounds each, their scales being as large as crown pieces. The Portuguese call them *moroes*. There is a saltwater creek that may be gone up three or four miles, to be near the freshwater watering place for ships, and every rock or stone, even the roots of the mangrove trees, affords a delicious small green oyster. Likewise, on the rocks at the seaside, there are sea-eggs, which resemble dock-burrs, but usually three or four times as large, of a sea-green or purple colour. In the inside they are divided into partitions, like oranges, each cell containing a yellow substance, which is eaten raw, and exceeds, in my opinion, all the shellfish I ever tasted. They also have prawns of extraordinary size, and we sometimes caught the sea horse in our nets. On the savannahs of Areziliba, on the continent opposite the southern end of St Catherine, they have great numbers of black cattle, some of which we had from them at a very reasonable price.

The Portuguese on St Catherine are a parcel of *banditti*, who have taken refuge here from the more strictly governed parts of Brazil. One Emanuel Mansa is captain-governor of the island. They enjoy the blessings of a fertile country and wholesome air, and need of nothing from other countries except clothing. They have sufficient firearms, and have often need of them, being greatly infected with tigers, ravenous animals which make great havoc. For this reason every house has many dogs, although I have been told that a tiger has killed eight or ten dogs in a night. But when any tigers make their appearance in the day, they seldom escape, as the inhabitants are fond of hunting them, and they are so numerous that it is quite common to see the prints of their paws on the sandy beach. As regards human habitation, we saw none of the fine dwelling-houses mentioned by earlier writers, nor any place could be called a town, nor any kind of fortification, except the woods, which, however, are a secure retreat from any enemy that may attack. I cannot say much about the Indians of those parts, as I never saw above two or three of them.

On Tuesday, 23 June, there being little wind, we got up to the main anchorage in St Catherine. I sent the carpenter ashore with all the crew that could be useful to him, to fell trees, and saw them into planks to repair our stern, while the cooper and his crew trimmed the water casks and filled them. Those aboard I employed in reorganising the stowing of the hold, to make room for our guns as we rounded Cape Horn, and to put into the meat casks a fresh supply of preservative pickle. The inhabitants of the island coming off daily with fresh provisions, to save our sea stores I bought twenty-one cattle, two hundred salted fish of large size, and 150 bushels of cassado meal. This is about as fine as our oatmeal, and from it a very hearty food is prepared with little trouble. I also bought 160 bushels of *calavances*, a small bean, for money at a dollar[34] the bushel, and partly in exchange for salt, measure for measure, and likewise I provided a quantity of tobacco for the crew.

On 2 July we saw a large ship at anchor about five miles away. After securing the watering place with two guns and sufficient men and ammunition I sent the launch, well-manned and armed, under a lieutenant, to see what she was. The launch returned about noon, reporting she was the *Ruby*, formerly an English man-of-war, but now in Martinet's squadron, and commanded by M La Jonquière. Her officers and crew were mostly French, to the number of about 420, though the ship was in the Spanish service. Yet they had no intention to molest us, having quitted the South Sea on report of a rupture between France and Spain. M La Jonquière was a man of strict honour, and next day, 3 July, proved his good intentions with an invitation to dinner. This I accepted, and was well entertained. But heard from him that the Spanish had been warned of the coming of our two ships, and were presently fitting out some of their men-of-war to receive us. I desired of him that this news be kept quiet, telling him that if my men heard anything that savoured of great difficulty, I should not have it in my power to make them proceed any further.

About this time, I heard that Hately had plundered the Portuguese ship we had met at Cape Frio of one hundred gold moidores, and had distributed part of the money among the boarding crew, to engage them to secrecy. I called him to strict account, when he told me he had done nothing in which he could not justify himself. I examined him closely, intending, if found guilty, to deliver him to Mansa, the captain-governor of St Catherine's, but I could not get sufficient proof. Hately also committed so many vile actions in the island of St Catherine that our people were often in the utmost danger from the resentments of the Portuguese. From the first day he outraged their women in the grossest manner; he and his gang threatening to ravish young and old. They also threatened to set their houses on fire, and did, in fact, burn one which the inhabitants had put aside for our use. But his bad conduct I could neither prevent nor punish, as he had become a great favourite with my mutinous crew.

On 6 July, M La Jonquière, with several of his officers and passengers, came to the *Speedwell* to dine with me. At the height of our mirth, Hudson, my boatswain, took it into his head to raise a mutiny. He claimed he had not had the respect due to him as I had not invited him into the great cabin to dine with us; also, that many lieutenants were deemed superior to him, while he should be rightly looked on as third man on the ship. To show how much he resented this imaginary ill-treatment, he resolved to destroy any gaiety being enjoyed by those who thought themselves so much above him, and was not long putting this into practice by assaulting Betagh, captain of marines, and Mr Adams, the surgeon.

This insolence being carried on in steerage, I stepped out of the cabin to see what might be the case for such a noise, and was surprised at the unparalleled impudence of him and his fellows, who accosted me with all manner of saucy expressions. But by the help of my officers and the French gentlemen, I soon drubbed them into better manners. When all was quiet, M la Jonquière now desired to speak to the crew. He told them that he and his officers were eyewitnesses, and if such disturbances continued he would offer to me to take the ringleaders home in irons, that my crew had great prospects in front of them to make their fortunes, and he mentioned that his own people were full of prize money, without half the encouragement that my crew had, and that there was not a man in his own ship who would not leave his wages to serve under me.

Next morning, I was informed most of the people were sorry, blaming everything on the boatswain, Hudson, and too much liquor. I passed it all over, only threatening how I would manage them if they were guilty of the like again. Hudson came to see me individually in humble plight, asking my pardon, begging I would not use any severity as drink had 'made him mad', etc., and would I allow him to go home in the French ship. I readily agreed, he being a very odd sort of fellow, always incensing the people against the officers, whom he termed 'bloodsuckers.'

On 15 July, we saw a large ship bearing in for the harbour, but on sighting us, she turned out again. This circumstance alarmed M La Jonquière who, suspecting she might be our consort, the *Success*, put to sea next morning.

And now a great heart-burning arose in my crew. Having heard in the past that crews on privateering voyages to the Great South Sea had been badly treated in regard in the distribution of prize money, they now, with the advice of Matthew Stewart, my chief mate, drew up a paper of articles respecting a new division of any plunder, insisting on these articles being made the rule of our voyage, to which, at last, I was obliged to agree, rather than suffer them to proceed in a piratical manner.

During all this, our carpenter and his men went on but slowly in the woods cutting up planks to repair our stern. He blamed the saw, but really they were idle. For my part, the only spur I had was to double their allowance of brandy, though they hardly deserved the water they drank. When we came to case over the stern, we found we had no nails, and I set the armourer to make some, which he did with the help of a forge and bellows given me by the captain of the *Ruby*. Upon enquiry, I learnt the original carpenter, who left the ship before it came to Plymouth, had sold most of the *Speedwell's* stores before he departed.

On 25 July we saw the same large ship coming in again under French colours. This was the *Wise Solomon*, of St Malo, who had now spoken to the *Ruby* at sea. The captain, M Girard Dumain, first abused M La Jonquière of the *Ruby*, calling him a renegade for serving under the Spanish flag, then defamed all earlier writers about the South Sea, saying all their books were full of the grossest errors: a designing, mercenary man, endued with all the conceit and vanity so natural to his nation. I desired he spare me some nails, as this was proving an endless task for my armourer, and he did so, selling them to me at thirty-two dollars per hundred.

I was now preparing for sea when there came a letter from the ship's company with articles attached, and threatening they would not stir a step to sea till what they demanded therein was securely agreed on. The letter, signed by my chief mate, Matthew Stewart, and eight more petty officers, and thirty-six chief foremast men, demanded that the monies, jewels, and cargoes of each prize taken be equally divided between the ship's company, as soon as possible after capture, according to each man's respective share as borne on the ship's books. And in return for my agreeing to this, 'Captain Shelvocke . . . shall have five per cent over and above his respective share.'

I learned Captain Hately tacitly approved of the plan, and on my opposing it, they sent Matthew Stewart to me with a letter giving him power of attorney and making him crew's agent, and begging they should have their shares of any fortune before it fell into the Gentlemen-Adventurers' hands, although stressing they would always do justice to these owners in England. After a few days more murmuring and uneasiness, and no work going forward, they all came onto the quarter-deck in a mutinous manner for my final resolution, clamouring in an outrageous manner against Mr Godfrey, the Gentlemen's principal agent on board, together with a thousand other scurrilous expressions which astonished me.

Finding them deaf to anything I urged, and thinking of my prospect of meeting Captain Clipperton in the South Seas and subduing them, and firmly believing they would do no less than run away with the ship if thwarted, thought it more advisable for the general good to sign, and if this might be thought a desperate remedy, it ought be looked on as being applied to a desperate disease!

2. The passage into the Great South Sea by the Straits of Le Maire. As we proceed south, appetites grow sharper and Betagh, my marine captain, becomes voracious and threatens me; I exclude him from my table. The seas full of great fish; we pass through the Straits of Le Maire and into the Pacific Ocean.

BUT TO GO ON with our voyage. We departed from the island of St Catherine on 9 August. I kept the lead constantly sounding all along the coast of Patagonia. From the latitude of 40° to 52° 30', both S, we saw great shoals of seals and penguins, which were always attended by flocks of pintadoes, birds about the size of pigeons. The French call them *damiers*, as their black and white feathers are disposed like the squares of a draughtboard. These were also attended by albatrosses, the largest of all seafowl, some extending their wings twelve or thirteen feet, tip to tip. While passing the mouth of the Rio de la Plata the sea was covered with prodigious quantities of large seaweed, which greatly incommoded us and deadened our way.

On getting farther south we saw an abundance of things floating on the surface of the sea, like white snakes. We took some up, but could not perceive them to have any appearance of life, being only a long cylinder of a white jelly-like substance, perhaps the

spawn of some large fish. As we advanced south, the
appetites of our crew increased with the sharpness of
the air; to the degree that the allowance which the
government gives the Navy was not sufficient to satisfy
their hunger. Some of my officers, one in particular, Mr
Betagh, my captain of marines, were very angry they
could not have their bellies full, or at least a greater
share than the common people of the crew, Betagh
saying, 'For what was my table if I did not eat better
than the cook?' To this I answered he fared as well as
myself, and without any charge to him. But he did not
think it proper to use any decency, and would sometime
take the greater part of what we had on his own plate.
He then used his endeavours to persuade the people,
'not to starve themselves' as he put it, and a little while
after I was forced to give them an extraordinary meal
every day of flour or beans, which greatly reduced our
stock of provisions, and consumed our wood and water.

Nor could Betagh stop here, but urged on by his
voracious appetite, had, at length, the insolence to
threaten me publicly that, 'the voyage should be short
with me,' a threat he often repeated, and which I should
have feared, had he been capable of command. For his
punishment I excluded him both from my table and the
great cabin. Anticipating a heavy punishment for his
mutinous behaviour, on 18 September 1719, he sent me
a letter asking my pardon and promising, 'never to
transgress in the same manner.' He added he felt I was

prepossessed in his disfavour for words he spoke to me 'seven or eight months gone.' And concluded that he was never a 'party man', and that he, and all others were satisfied, 'since the late amendment of the prize and plunder money.' From this, it may be seen that this was not the first crime of which he had been guilty, but hearing he was prepared to confess his sins openly, I restored him in a handsomer manner than he deserved, as will appear by the sequel.

To resume the thread of our voyage, I must inform the reader that whales, grampuses, and other fish of monstrous size are in such vast numbers on the coast of Patagonia that they were often offensive to us, coming so close to us that it seemed impossible to avoid striking them on every scud of a sea, and almost stifling us with the stench of their breaths when they blew close to windward. Being ignorant of the Greenland whaling fishery, I cannot pretend to say whether that trade might not be carried on here, but this I may venture to affirm that the navigation here is safer, and I am apt to believe it has a greater chance of being successful.

On 19 September, about midnight, perceiving the water all at once to be discoloured, we sounded twenty-five fathoms, and therefore stood out from the land, but did not deepen our water in fifteen miles. This bank must lie very near the entrance into the Straits of Magellan. But having no chart that described the coast (for Clipperton, who was supplied with everything necessary of this kind, for both ships, did not think for to let me have any) we now steered for the Straits of Le Maire, and met with very foggy weather on approaching the coast of Tierra del Fuego. I had a fine opportunity of going through the Straits of Magellan, but Captain Clipperton had pretended to me that the Straits of Le Maire would be the best navigation, though he himself used the Straits of Magellan, from which it may be conjectured he designed this as another expedient to separate himself from us, and I shall show in its proper place he was a man who would do anything rather than not follow his own inclinations, be they never so dishonest or inhuman.

The fog cleared up on the 23 September, when we had sight of stupendous mountains on Tierra del Fuego, entirely covered with snow. But before we could ascertain our situation, the mist returned and I stood off for some time and then brought to. At four next morning, proceeding under easy sail to the southeast, it proved very clear at daybreak, and we now had a full, but melancholy, prospect of the most desolate country that can well be conceived, appearing as chains upon chains of mountains, one behind the other, and perpetually clothed in snow.

Hitherto we had not been sensible of any current, either favourable or adverse, after passing the Rio de la Plata. But that afternoon we were hurried with incredible rapidity into the Straits of Le Maire, the tide slackening once we had gained about the middle of the passage, and sounding twenty-seven fathoms on a rocky bottom. Now the return tide rushed upon us with a violence equal to that which brought us in, and with astonishing rapidity we were driven again north, even though we had a fresh gale at northwest, and we were carried quite out of the straits to the north in about an hour. Upon this shift of tide there arose such a short sea, and so lofty at the same time, that we alternately dipped our bowsprit and poop lanterns into the water, our ship all the while labouring most violently, and refusing to answer the helm. The tide shifted again at midnight, and again we shot through the Straits, steering south with a brisk gale at northwest without seeing the land distinctly on either side, and, in the morning, had progressed well to southward.

Cold before, it now became extreme. The bleak westerly winds had of themselves been sufficiently piercing, but these were now always accompanied by snow or sleet, which beat continually on our sails and rigging, and cased in all our masts, yards, and ropes with ice. And we were beset with so severe storms, that we thought the weather tolerable when we could carry a reefed mainsail, lying-to for days under bare poles, exposed to the shocks of prodigious waves, more mountainous than any I had ever seen.

We now felt the benefit of our awning we had rigged, without which we could scarcely have lived. The wind continued to rage without intermission from the westward, by which we were driven down to the latitude of 61° 30' S, and had such mist, that we were under perpetual apprehension of running foul of ice islands. The winds by themselves would have been sufficiently piercing, but being always attended by snow and sleet, which continually beating on our sails and rigging cased the masts and every rope in ice in manner that rendered them useless to us. Though the days were long, we could seldom get sight of the sun, so that we had only one observation in all this passage, which was in latitude 60° 37' S, 5° to the westward of the Straits of Le Maire, when we found it 22° 6' NE.

On Thursday, 1 October 1719, at seven in the evening, as we were furling the mainsail, one William Camell cried out that his hands and fingers were so benumbed that he could not hold himself, but, before those near could assist him, he fell and was drowned.

The cold is certainly more insupportable in these than in the same latitudes to north, for though we were pretty well advanced in the summer season and the days were long, we were subjected to continual squalls of sleet, snow and rain, while the heavens were hidden under perpetual dismal clouds. In short, one would think it impossible that anything living could subsist in such a climate, and we all observed that we had not the sight of one fish since we had come southward of the Straits of Le Maire, nor one seabird excepting a disconsolate black albatross who accompanied us for several days, hovering about us as if he had lost himself. Hately, observing in one of his melancholy fits that this bird, from his colour, might be of some ill omen, was encouraged in this superstition by a never-ending contrary tempestuous winds; and so, after some fruitless attempts, he at length shot the albatross not doubting (perhaps) we should have a fair wind after that.

I must own that this navigation into the Great South Sea, is, in truth, melancholy. More so as without our consort, the *Success*, we, as it were, had to struggle far from the rest of mankind without any friendly port to recourse to in case of loss of masts or other accident, and without chance of receiving assistance from any other vessel. But the hopes of enjoying a long repose in the Pacific Sea, on the coasts of Peru, lighted our cares and gave us some small relief.

On 22 October, at eight at night, our fore-topmast was carried away, and we rigged another next day. Having contrary winds from the time we passed the Straits of Le Maire, with the most uncomfortable weather, we made our way very slowly to the west and north, the hopes of getting soon into a warmer and better climate supporting us under our many miseries.

Saturday, 14 November 1719: at noon we saw the coast of Chile, bearing northeast by east, distance ten leagues, latitude per observation, 47° 28' S. We had now arrived truly into the Great South Sea.

3. We proceed to the isle of Chiloe to take provisions; burn two prizes at Conception for lack of payment of ransoms; call at Juan Fernández to attempt a rendezvous with the *Success* and Captain Clipperton.

OUR SPIRITS NOW cheered by being on the coast of Chile, yet here we still found ourselves under very great difficulties. Our slow passage, and extraordinary consumption of provisions, had so reduced our wood, water, and food, that it was now necessary to find some place where our wants might be supplied.

We first tried Narborough Island, but finding the anchorage unsafe, sailed for the mouth of St Domingo river on the continent, where we had twenty-eight fathoms, shoaling as we advanced from eighteen, to less than five, as fast as a man could heave the lead. Finding this place also too hazardous, we stood out to sea, and were blown farther north than we designed. Being greatly at a loss where to procure wood and water, one Joseph de La Fontaine, a Frenchman, proposed going to the island of Chiloe (42°S 73°W) assuring us that the towns of Chacao and Calibuco, the former on the island, and the latter on the continent, were rich places, where we could not fail of procuring whatever we wanted. Chacao was, he said, the usual residence of the governor, while at Calibuco was a wealthy college of

Jesuits, well-stocked with provisions of all kinds. This person at the same time insinuated among the crew, that our expedition would probably turn out unfortunate, if we passed this place, as Captain Clipperton must by this time have alarmed the whole of the west coast of South America, in consequence of which there would now be warships waiting for us further north. This, in a manner, fitting in with my own thoughts, induced me to make an attempt on Chiloe to procure provisions. If the coast were alarmed, we could then retire to some unfrequented island, till the Spaniards should suppose we had abandoned the South Sea.

Accordingly, on Monday, 30 November 1719, we entered the channel which divides the island of Chiloe from the mainland of Chile; and, having hoisted French colours, stood in for the harbour of Chacao, intending to take it by surprise. Our French pilot, however, seemed as much a stranger to the navigation here as I was, and as the wind began to blow fresh, at ten in the morning, I came to anchor in thirteen fathoms near the small island of Pedro Núñez. Soon after, the tide made outwards with prodigious rapidity, the wind increased greatly, the sea became very boisterous, and all the channel appeared one continued breach or surf. Our ship, consequently, made a vast strain on her cable, which parted at two in the afternoon, losing our anchor. I did not think it advisable to risk another anchor, and therefore immediately crossed over for the island of

Chiloe, in a boisterous gale with thick rainy weather, surrounded on all hands with seeming shoals, and bewildered in an unknown navigation.

Keeping off about a mile from the coast of Chiloe, we ranged along the shore in hope of discovering the town of Chacao. We passed two commodious bays, with no appearance of any town, and came to a point of land marked by a high pyramidal rock. After getting round, we found ourselves entirely out of the tideway, and quite sheltered from all other inconveniences, and came therefore to anchor, having just sufficient daylight to enable us to get into this place of shelter.

Next morning, I sent the second lieutenant, in the pinnace, well-manned and armed, to look for the town, and at the same time Mr Hately, in the launch, to endeavour to find a watering place. He soon returned accompanied by an Indian, who had shown him a very convenient place to procure both wood and water, that was even under the command of our guns from the ship, and therefore free from all danger of being surprised. I accordingly manned and armed the launch and sent it with casks to be filled, together with an officer of marines and ten men to keep guard. The Indian gave us hopes of a sufficient supply of provisions, but he came in the evening to our crew onshore, to acquaint them that the governor had forbidden the natives to bring, or sell, anything to us. As the pinnace had not yet returned, this information gave me much concern, fearing that the enemy had taken her, and now learnt what we were.

On the 3 December 1719, about seven in the evening, a Spanish officer, being sent by the governor of Chiloe, came to us in a boat rowed by eight Indians. Already flying French colours, and meaning to pass for a French captain well known in these seas, I ordered none of my crew to appear on deck but such as could speak that language, or Spanish. When the officer came on board, I told him my ship was the *St Rose*, homeward-bound, that my name was Janis le Breton, and that I entreated the governor to spare me what provisions he could conveniently afford, that being my only business on the coast. The officer heard me with much civility, seeming to credit all I said, even staid on board all night, and went away next morning, to all appearance well satisfied.

On 5 December, in the morning, two boats came towards us full of armed men, but, after taking a view of us, went to a small island in the mouth of the harbour. On the 6th we saw a white flag hoisted ashore. I sent my launch, completely manned and armed, but they found no person near the flag, just a letter attached to its shaft, with a dozen hams lying close by. The letter was from Don Nicholas Salvo, governor of Chiloe, doubting strongly of our ship being the *St Rose*, complaining of the behaviour of the people in our pinnace, and desiring me to leave the coast.

I returned an answer in as proper terms as I could devise, and next morning had another letter, couched in the utmost civility, but absolutely refusing me any refreshments, and demanding the restitution of the Indians made prisoners by our pinnace. Of course, I knew less of our pinnace than he did, and believed that he actually had the pinnace and its people already in his hands. Despairing of ever seeing my pinnace crew again, and still ignorant as to where Chacao was situated, I determined to change my style of writing, and try what could be done by threatening force.

I therefore wrote that I was determined to have provisions by fair means or foul, and next day sent my first lieutenant, Mr Brooks, in the launch with twenty-nine well-armed men, ordering him to bring off all he could find. Shortly after, a boat came with a message from the governor, offering to treat with me, if I would send an officer to Chacao. I answered, that I would treat nowhere but on board, and that he was now too late, as I had already sent eighty men on shore to take all they could find. In the evening Mr Brooks and the launch returned, accompanied by a large piragua, or native canoe, both completely laden with sheep, hogs, fowls, barley, and green peas and beans.

Soon afterwards, the pinnace arrived with all her crew, behaving in a terrified manner; the officer telling me he had been forced to fight his way past Chacao through several canoes filled with armed Indians, before finding it necessary to make a passage quite round the island, in order to escape, a journey of not less than 350 miles. This story, I found, proceeded only from excess of terror, as they only met one boat with unarmed Indians and a Spanish sergeant, who came offshore to them without the least show of violence. The only excuse the officer then alleged was that the tide had hurried him away, and he forgot in his fright that he had a grappling in the boat, with which he might have anchored till the tide turned. In short, their dread was so great than rather pass back by the town of Chacao again (even at night) they chose rather to row round so great an island in a small open boat crowded with as many men as she could well carry, in climate subject to hard gales of wind, and with as dangerous seas as off the coasts of England. So that it was a hundred to one they were not lost. Seeing them all confounded with shame, I said but little to them, and only made the officer who commanded them sensible of his unpardonable mismanagement.

By this strange affair I missed a favourable opportunity of seizing Chacao within forty-eight hours after our arrival, when the governor was totally unprepared. But now, having had a whole week, he had collected near a thousand armed Spaniards, as I learnt from an Indian who had been taken prisoner in the pinnace. I therefore laid aside all thoughts of taking Chacao, and decided we would furnish ourselves from the Indian farms and plantations prior to sailing.

Therefore, on 11 December I sent the pinnace ashore

with a bill written in Spanish to be fixed to the door of
some remarkable Indian house, whereby I gave them
to understand they had no one to blame for any
hostilities committed on them but the governor who
was preventing them bringing us provisions to sell at
their own price. But as I must have provisions, they
could either leave out for me four hams, four bushels of
wheat, and a quantity of potatoes, and they would
sustain no loss. Otherwise I would burn their houses
and all their standing corn, and commit all the
outrages I could devise.

The Spaniards saw to it that this should have no effect
on the natives, but I was supplied tolerably well by my
own people foraging ashore who proceeded with
diligence and good order in that respect, but proved sad
fellows in others, as in the person of Betagh, whom I sent
onshore with a party to see what service he could do with
them. But as soon as the pinnace landed, he called to his
sergeant, 'Damn Captain Shelvocke! Why did he send
me with these people?', and gave over the command to
the sergeant, while Betagh himself retired into the ranks.
This made the people entertain a mean opinion of their
land commander, and on preparing to return to the
Speedwell, and having difficulty shipping what they had
taken, they asked Betagh to assist. He refused and they
left him onshore, where he stayed all night.

I asked Hately how he could treat his brother officer
with so much disrespect, and he answered that as

Betagh would not deign to wet his feet, and none of the crew would carry him into a boat already over-burdened, they said they would not load themselves with one who was neither seaman nor soldier. Betagh laid the whole blame on Hately for this incident, and threatened to use him very roughly if he ever met him ashore. To prevent which, ever after when they went ashore on business together, Hately always took care to be boatkeeper.

By 16 December 1719, our decks were full of live cattle, and poultry, and hams in abundance, together with such quantities of wheat, barley, potatoes, and maize, that on a moderate computation we had added four months' provisions to the stock we brought from England. Well-pleased with the effects of our stay at Chiloe, I now prepared to depart. But might certainly have done much more for my own credit, and the profit of my owners, had it not been for the mismanagement of the officer in the pinnace.

On leaving Chiloe I reflected that the soil of this island is very fertile, producing all sorts of European fruits and grains, and it has fine pasture lands, with great numbers of cattle and particularly sheep. The air is wholesome and temperate, yet I suspect the winters may be rigorous, being bounded on the west by an immense ocean, and without any land screen from the tempestuous westerly winds. There are also in this island an abundance of very handsome middle-sized horses, which the natives manage with great dexterity. They have also an animal, called *guanaco* or llama, or *carneso de tierra*, that is, sheep of the country, which very much resembles a camel, but not nearly so large. These have long necks, and are between five and six feet high. Their wool or soft hair is very fine, but they smell very rank, and have a slow majestic pace, which hardly any violence can make them quicken, yet they are of great service at the mines in Peru, where they are employed in carrying the ore and other things. Their flesh is very coarse, as we experienced, having salted some of them for our future use. Besides these, are great numbers of hogs, but not many black cattle, though the island has plenty of fowls, both wild and tame. Among the former is a small species of goose, beautifully white, and of excellent taste. The tame poultry are the same kinds with our own.

The natives are in almost all respects the same with those on the continent of Chile, of moderate stature, with deep olive complexions, and coarse shaggy black hair, some with by no means disagreeable features. They seem naturally of fierce and warlike dispositions, but the oppressions of the Spaniards, and the artifices of the Jesuits, who are the missionaries in these parts, have curbed and broken their spirits. Frézier in his writings says that the Indians on the continent, to the southward of this island, are called Chonos, who go quite naked, and that there is a race of men of extraordinary size in the inland parts of the country, called Cacahues, some of which were about nine or ten feet high. I had sight of two of these Indians, who came from the southward of St Domingo river, who did not seem to me to differ in their persons from the ordinary natives of Chiloe. They were decently clothed in ponchos, *monteras*, and *poulains*. The poncho is a sort of square carpet, having a slit or hole cut in the middle, wide enough to slip over the head, so that it hangs down over the shoulders, half before and half behind, under which they generally wear a short doublet. The *montera* is a cap, nearly like those of our postillions, and their legs are covered by the *poulains*, a kind of hose without feet. In short, their appearance has little or none of the savage. Their habitations are firmly built of planks, but have no chimneys, so that they are very black and sooty within.

They enclose some of their land for cultivation, with rails or palings, and although they have plenty of everything necessary to a comfortable subsistence, they have no bread, from wanting mills in which to grind and prepare their wheat. They use a miserable substitute, a kind of cake of seaweeds, which is much esteemed by them, and even liked by some of our men. Besides this, they prepare their maize in several manners to answer the purpose of bread, and they use potatoes and other roots with the same intention.

Their liquor is called *chicha*, made from their Indian

corn, but the Spaniards endeavour to curb them in this, as their drinking bouts have often occasioned revolts. Such of the natives as have no European weapons use pikes or darts. Among the other arms of the country is a running noose on a long leathern thong, called a *lays*, or lasso, which they use with surprising dexterity for catching cattle, horses, or other animals, even when at full career. There is a small woollen manufacture, consisting of ponchos and other articles of clothing formerly mentioned. They also export considerable quantities of cedar, both in plank, and wrought up into boxes, chests, desks, and the like, with which they supply all Chile and Peru.

They have no European trade, but a Spaniard who came to me from the governor expressed his astonishment that no ships ever put in, saying they had plenty of money among them, with a safe port, free from danger, where a great deal of business might be done here, before news could reach Lima and warships be fitted out and sent so great a way to windward.

It is observed of the Chiloese, that, differing from all other nations ever heard of, they have no notion of a supreme being, and consequently have no kind of worship, and are such enemies to civil society that they never live together in towns and villages, so that their country seems thinly inhabited, though very populous, the whole nation being dispersed in farms at a good distance, every family having its own plantation, and raising its own necessaries. Though scattered, they are not wholly independent, each tribe being subject to a chief, called a cacique, whose dwelling is conveniently situated among them for speedily summoning them together, done by the sound of a sort of horn. This chief commands them in war, and has an absolute power of dispensing justice among his subjects, who all consider themselves as his relations, he being as it were the head of his family, and his authority hereditary. In these respects, the inhabitants of Chiloe resemble their neighbours on the continent, excepting that their caciques are stripped in a great measure of their power and influence by the tyranny of the Spaniards, who keep them under the most servile slavery, while the missionaries blind them by a superstitious and imperfect conversion to Christianity, of which not one of these natives know anything more than merely that they were baptised, all their devotion consisting of mere idolatry of the cross, or the images of saints. For the Jesuits use no manner of pains to enlighten their minds, but think it better, by keeping them in ignorance, to make them more contented under the rigorous government of the Spaniards.

Under this delusion, the caciques have changed their lawful powers for the vain ostentation of being allowed to carry a silver-headed cane, outwardly placing them on a footing with a Spanish captain. Yet have they sometimes rebelled against their proud oppressors, deeming death preferable to slavery, as may be seen in the account of Frézier's voyage.

The vessels used in Chiloe are peculiarly constructed, as, for want of nails and other articles of iron, the planks of which their boats are constructed are sewed together with reeds. These boats are constructed of three pieces only, the keel or bottom being one piece, and the sides two others. They are rowed with oars, in the same manner as with us, more or fewer according to their size.

I sailed from Chiloe with design to go straight to the island of Juan Fernández for another possible rendezvous with Captain Clipperton as directed in my instructions, but my men took it into their heads that great things might be done in the Bay of Conception (36° 50' S) to which also they were induced by the same Frenchman who persuaded us to come to Chiloe. He pretended that there were always five or six ships in the road of Conception, besides others daily coming in and out, and that these had often considerable sums of money or silver, with other valuable things on board, and that though large ships, they carried few guns, and neither were there any fortifications at that place, so that we could not meet any opposition, even if there were twenty sail. He said their cargoes consisted chiefly of corn, wine, brandy, and jerked beef, and that ships bound for Conception always brought money to purchase their cargoes, and carried, besides, rich passengers who carry on a considerable trade over land between Conception and Buenos Aires, and who, together with any ships we took, might be ransomed. He also alleged that we should certainly make our fortunes, if we could only reach Conception before they had notice of our being in these seas. This man, who was now behaving as the only one who could instruct us in to how to make our fortunes, therefore advised my crew to prevail on me to make the best of my way to Conception before the governor of Chiloe could alarm the coast, and we should have no opportunity of meeting with anything till the Spaniards imagined we were gone from the South Sea.

In these cases, as all are fond of delivering their sentiments, and as it is impossible to keep a ship's company much in awe in remote parts, my men did not fail to speak their minds somewhat insolently. One William Morphew, who had been in these seas several years, took upon him to tell me, that it did not signify much if we arrived two or three days sooner or later at Juan Fernández. He said also, that I was a stranger here, but the Frenchman and he were well acquainted with these seas, and everybody hoped I would not put a mere obedience to orders, against so fair prospects as we would find in Conception. In short, though they assured they would all sooner rather perish than injure our gentlemen-owners in any respect, they entreated me not to let slip this opportunity, in which they would stand by me with all fidelity.

On our way to Conception, we made the islands of Mocha and St Mary on 23 December 1719, and arrived that same evening in the Bay of Conception. I immediately gave Hately orders to man and arm our boats, and sent them upriver that same night, in order to surprise any ships that might be there. I added that if the ships they found were too strong, to prevent those vessels from sending anything onshore until I were able to work the *Speedwell* up. This latter I endeavoured to do all night, but to little purpose, as at daylight I could discern nothing above us.

Captain Hately returned about noon of the 24th, informing me that he had taken a ship of about 150 tons, lately arrived from Baldivia, but having only a few cedar planks on board, and no persons but the boatswain, an old negro, and two Indian boys. He had left her in the charge of Mr Brooks, my first lieutenant, with orders to bring her down at the first opportunity. On his way back he had taken another small vessel, of about twenty-five tons, carrying pears, cherries, and other fruits to sell at Conception. This vessel belonged to a priest who we now made prisoner in her. Watching Hately coming back with the prize through my telescope, I had perceived another small boat come within a pistol-shot of him in the pinnace, and yet Captain Hately did not engage her. His excuse, after he came on board, was that he did not see her, though our boat's crew said she was full of men. This vessel I believed had come from Chiloe bringing news of us. This was the most stupid neglect on the part of Hately that could be conceived.

26 December 1719: the priest, solicitous to ransom his bark, left the ship about seven in the morning to go ashore to raise the money for the purpose. About noon, Mr Brooks brought down the prize, the *Solidad*, anchoring half a mile short of us. The boatswain of this prize had not been two hours in the *Speedwell*, till he told us of a vessel, laden with wine, brandy, and other valuable things, riding at anchor in the Bay of Herradura, about six miles north of us. Receiving this information, I ordered Mr Randal, my second lieutenant, with twenty-five men, to go in the *Mercury* (which we had renamed the priest's fruit bark) and, accompanied by the Spanish boatswain, to go in search of this vessel in the Bay of Herradura, with *positive* orders not to land or to make any other hazardous attempt.

Next evening they returned with the following melancholy story. On getting into the bay, they found the vessel hauled ashore, so Randal ordered his crew to land and bring away what they could find, while he and three or four more kept the *Mercury* afloat. The crew found the would-be prize empty, but seeing a small house hard by, on top of a bank, suspected her cargo might be lodged there. An inferior officer who was with them ordered them to search this house. So they went accordingly, with each endeavouring to be foremost. But on reaching the top of the bank, they discovered the enemy coming furiously towards them. Some of the seamen were of opinion that they all might have escaped had they not been astonished at the strange manner in which they were attacked, by a number of horses galloping at them without riders. This caused some to stand amazed, but then seeing the danger, bestirred themselves to make the best of their way to the *Mercury*, the Spaniards coming after them in the following singular manner. First came the riderless horses, two abreast, and linked together. Behind came the Spanish on horseback, lying on the necks of their horses, and driving the others before them, not being seen to sit up on their saddles, except to fire their muskets.

When they got near our people, they threw their *lays*, or lassos, and accordingly ensnared James Daniel, a foremast man, who was a good way into the water, and whom they dragged out again, as he said, at the rate of ten knots. The Spaniards in Chile are universally dexterous in the use of this running noose, for I have seen a Spaniard bring a man up by the foot as he ran along the deck, and they are sure of any thing they fling at, at the distance of several fathoms. In all, five of my men were made prisoners. Fortunately for the others, the *Mercury* had, by some accident, got aground, or they must all have been cut off as the Spaniards thought fit to retire on finding themselves within musket-range of the *Mercury*. The *Mercury* was got afloat, but as the water was low, they were obliged in going out of the bay to keep very near a point of land, from which the Spaniards peppered them. But, by lying in the bottom of the ship, on this occasion only one man was wounded, shot through the thigh.

These disappointments made my crew extremely uneasy, damning the South Seas and saying that if this was making a fortune they had better have stayed at home and begged about the streets. And there might well have been bad consequences, if we had not been agreeably surprised by seeing a large ship coming round Quiri-quinie, a small island in the entrance of the Bay of Conception. It was by this time almost dark, so that her people could not perceive what we were, and she stood towards us without fear, and we took her without resistance, being, as we always were, cleared and ready for action.

She proved to be the *St Fermin*, of about 300 tons, from Callao, with a cargo of sugar, molasses, rice, coarse French linen, some woollen cloth, and bays from Quito, a small quantity of chocolate, and about five or six thousand dollars in money and wrought plate. I sent Mr Hendry, the owners' agent, to inspect her cargo, and bring everything of value out of her into the *Speedwell*, and the ship's company sent their agent, Matthew Stewart, likewise. They returned with bales, boxes, chests, portmanteaus, and other packages, and a large quantity of sugar, molasses, and chocolate, and about seventy hundred weight of good rusk, with all her other stores and eatables. Don Francisco Larragan, the captain of the *St Fermin*, begged to be allowed to ransom her, which I willingly consented to, and allowed him to go in his own launch to Conception to raise the money, accompanied by a merchant, one of the prisoners. In the meantime, the *St Fermin*, was busily searched, lest any thing might have been concealed, but everyone who came at any time from her was also strictly searched by some of our own crew appointed for the purpose, that none might appropriate any thing of value.

On 30 December, an officer came offshore with a flag of truce from Don Gabriel Cano, the governor of Conception, who told us that two of our crew, taken in the late skirmish, were still alive, but very much wounded. This officer also brought a present of seven jars of very good wine, and a letter from the governor, in which he demanded to see my commission, and some other things I thought unreasonable, engaging to enter into a treaty, if I would comply with these requests. At length a formal treaty was begun, in which I demanded sixteen thousand dollars for the ransom of the *St Fermin*. After a further exchange of politenesses, on 1 January 1720, I sent Captain Betagh to the governor with a copy of my commission. All that day the enemy posted themselves along the shore, firing guns. I was no less vigilant, and every one-and-a-half hours during the night we beat three ruffs on the drums and gave three

'Huzzas'. For further security I spread a net of seven foot
deep above the gunwale from the main shrouds. I also
kept slowly under weigh when we had wind, and when
we had none extended out the ship's oars out to serve as
so many booms to prevent us being boarded and set on
fire. At midnight they fired twelve guns, and soon after
Betagh returned with a Flemish Jesuit, a Spanish lawyer,
an Englishman and a Scotsman. I immediately showed
my commission to the Englishman who read it in
Spanish to them, after which the Jesuit revealed that
though his profession was spiritual, he was quite willing
to indulge in temporal affairs, coming to acquaint me
that the governor, and the captains of the *St Fermin* and
Solidad had resolved to give me twelve thousand dollars
for both ships, the *Solidad* and the *St Fermin*, plus the
Mercury, rather then the sixteen thousand I wanted for
the *St Fermin* alone. I answered that no persuasions,
artifice or pretence would make me agree to it, and the
night was spent in fruitless discussion.

The Jesuit, however, had an affair of his own, which
was no doubt the chief reason he chose to put himself
amongst us. Out of the *St Fermin* we had taken ten large
silver candlesticks, each of which weighed about
twenty-five pounds sterling, and now the holy father
broke off from the ransom discussions to humbly beg
me to make him a present of these candlesticks which
he represented were a legacy left his convent, and hoped
I would now put them in the possession of those for

whom they were designed. He informed me it would be a deed of the highest merit, and would lay him and his brethren under the strictest obligations to send up prayers for my success in all my undertakings. This return seemed very inconsistent with reason that they should pray for a happy issue to the undertakings of one whose business was to do all the damage possible to the good father's fellow subjects, and to the open ruin of such Spaniards who fell into my hands. Thinking to oblige him, I offered them to him for their weight in dollars, a very advantageous bargain considering the price paid in those parts for wrought plate.

He declined, and we returned to the subject of the *St Fermin*. And I offered this ship and the *Solidad* for sixteen thousand dollars, but added that after twenty-four hours, if I had heard nothing, they should lose both ships. At six in the morning they left. Two days later still nothing had yet been heard, but on 4 January my wounded men came off (after being stripped while passing through the town) with a letter from the Governor saying the captain of the *St Fermin* would pay twelve thousand dollars, but wanted me to sent ashore two of my officers as hostages for it, together with the chaplain of the *St Fermin* whom I was holding as hostage. Word also came that the captain of the *St Fermin* would have sent the ransom money forty-eight hours ago, but the governor would not permit him. Realising that the governor's triflings and his letters full of the grossest falsehoods were intended only to entrap us, I set fire to the *Solidad*. Next day a letter came asking again for me to send two officers as hostages, to send back the prisoners I had on board, and to take twelve thousand dollars for the *St Fermin*, saying it would be of no advantage to me to lose such a sum.

To this I replied I had acted handsomely to everyone concerned, that I would not send any of my officers onshore, amongst plotters and contrivers, and if the money did not arrive at noon I would infallibly burn the *St Fermin*. The next day, a fifth and last letter came, restating all of the foregoing, and asking for another day. I gave him until the following noon, and on 6 January the morning passed without any news. Noon being lapsed, I made preparations on the *Speedwell* for sailing. At the same time I unfurled all the sails on the *St Fermin*, and hoisting a Spanish jack at her foremast, and a Spanish ensign at the main topmast head, and nothing happening from the town, I ordered her to be set on fire (whose cotton sails being loosed made a prodigious blaze).

This being done, I immediately got under weigh, being much chagrined at the loss of so many days to the perfidious delusions of the governor, but with the satisfaction that I had not sent any of my people ashore as hostage who would have been kept there, making me stay in port until the governor had time to gather reinforcements from neighbouring ports. I hoped my actions would alarm the coast to ransom without delay, and later learned that if they had believed I would have destroyed the *St Fermin* they would have given twenty to thirty thousand dollars to have saved her, being one of the best sailers, and fitted-out, of all Peruvian traders. She was a ship that would have cost ninety or one hundred thousand pieces of eight to build, while the price I had asked was what they would have paid to have her careened at Callao.

With the *Mercury*, we had sailed from Conception on 7 January 1720, intending for Juan Fernández, to try for news of the *Success*, and on the 8th observed the sea to be an entirely red colour, occasioned, as the Spaniards say, by the spawn of some large fish.

On 9 January, the plunder taken in the *St Fermin* was sold by the ship's agent, Matthew Stewart, at an onboard auction, and brought extravagant prices. The account being taken, and the shares calculated, the crew insisted on an immediate distribution. This was done, and each foremast-man had the rate of ten dollars a share, in money and goods. On 11 January we saw the island of Juan Fernández, having travelled 360 miles from Conception.

The island of Juan Fernández is in latitude 33° 40' S and longitude 79° W, being at the distance of about 150 marine leagues, or 450 miles, or 7° 30' from the coast of Chile. It is about fifteen English miles long from east to west and five miles at the broadest, from north to south, entirely composed of mountains and valleys, so that there is no walking a quarter of a mile on the flat. The anchoring place is on the north side of the island, and is distinguished by a little mountain, with a high peak on each side. It is not safe to anchor in less than forty fathoms, and even there, ships are very much exposed to sharp gales from the north, which blow frequently. There cannot be a more unpleasant place to anchor in, as the bay is surrounded by high mountains, and is subject to alternate dead calms and sudden stormy gusts of wind.

On entering the roads, I immediately sent the *Mercury* ashore, to have her leaks stopped, while I, until 15 January, stood off and on, while using the *Speedwell*'s small boats for fishing, catching so many that we salted five barrels. Once ashore, I could find no marks of Captain Clipperton having been here, but at length some of my men saw the words 'Magee' and 'Captain John' cut upon a tree. Magee was the name of Clipperton's surgeon, but as no directions were left for me, as agreed in instructions, it was evident he never meant I should join him again. We therefore prepared to continue our cruise.

4. We cruise Arica and the Vale of Arica.
We take two prizes and see the curious craft
called the *Balsa*; Captains Hately and Betagh
are captured by the Spanish. I take and burn
the town of Payta. We are wrecked on the isle
of Juan Fernández.

NOW KNOWING Captain Clipperton was somewhere in
the South Sea, I made the best of my way from Juan
Fernández, being well-provisioned, and with all our
water casks filled. On 21 January 1720, with the design
of looking into Copiapo, I put Mr Dodd, second
lieutenant of marines, into the *Mercury*, with eight men,
and sent her next evening to cruise close to the land,
while I kept the *Speedwell* out of sight in the offing. On
this occasion, I took care to give the officer commanding
Mercury a copy of my commission, with all necessary
instructions how to proceed, appointing the headland
of Copiapo to be our place of meeting. The business of
the *Mercury* was to look into the port of Copiapo, called
Caldera (27° S 70° 50' W), where there are some gold
mines, and a considerable export of that metal in small
vessels. The *Mercury*, having the advantage of being
Chilean-built, would hopefully not excite suspicion.

Next day I hove in towards Copiapo, but lay to the
southward, that I might not be seen from the port.
While here, opposite a small island which lies athwart

the mouth of the Copiapo river, I sent the pinnace to fish between that isle and the mainland, and soon after saw a vessel crowding all sail towards us. It was the *Mercury*, whose officer told me he had looked into the port, but could see no shipping. But he had looked into a wrong place, and having made him sensible of his error, I sent him again to the right place, about six leagues farther north. Next morning our fishing pinnace returned, bringing only a few penguins which she had taken on the island in the bay of Copiapo. The *Mercury* had looked into Caldera, but saw nothing, and instead of making use of the land wind to come off to me, had kept along shore in the bottom of the bay till the land wind came in so strong that she was nearly lost on the lee shore.

On the 27th, I sent Mr Brooks, my first lieutenant, and Mr Rainor, first lieutenant of marines, to relieve Mr Randal and Mr Dodd in the *Mercury*, which I had fitted with a gang of oars, and, upon trial, she was found to make way at the rate of three knots, which might render her extremely useful in a calm. On 5 February, I dispatched Mr Brooks ahead in the *Mercury*, to see if there were any ships in the harbour of Arica (lat. 18° 26' S) and next day I got sight of the headland of Arica, with a ship at anchor on its northern side. I saw the *Mercury* standing out of the bay, by which I judged the ship was too warm for her, and therefore made all haste to get up with the *Speedwell*. On coming up, we found

77

that the ship was already taken, and the *Mercury* accidentally adrift.

This prize was called the *Rosario*, of 100 tons, laden with cormorants' dung, which the Spanish call guano, and is brought from Iquique to use in the culture of the cod pepper, or capsicum, from which they make a vast profit in the vale of Arica. In the *Rosario* there was no white face but the pilot, whom I sent ashore to see if the owner wished to ransom her and her cargo, the guano being worth gold to them, but useless to us. Next morning I received a letter from Miguel Diaz Gonzale, owner of the ship, insisting pitifully on his poverty and distress, having a large family to provide for, and promising to meet secretly that night to treat for a ransom. We soon after took a small bark, further laden with guano, and some dried fish.

By this time, all the adjacent country was up in arms about us, and great numbers came down to the coast, well-mounted and seemingly well-disciplined. To try their courage, I ordered the *Mercury*, and the launch, to draw near the shore, as if we intended to land, though the landing place here is altogether imprac-ticable. I also cannonaded the town briskly. Our balls made no execution, just ploughed up the sand in front of the Spanish horses, throwing it all over them. But neither this, nor the approach of my small craft, made any impression, for they stood firm, and showed the countenance of being as good troops as could be wished.

This disappointed me, as it showed my men the Spaniards were far from being the cowards they had been represented.

As soon as it was dark, Gonzales came off to me, and I agreed to let him have back the *Rosario*, and the six negroes in her, for 1,500 dollars, reserving right to take anything out of her that might be useful. At ten next night he brought me the agreed sum, 1,300 dollars in ingots of virgin silver, called *pinnas*, and the rest in coined dollars. He also made great enquiry for English commodities, for which he offered high prices, complaining that the French supplied them with paltry goods, but for which they charged vast sums. He added, that he supposed the English merchants were all asleep, or too rich, as they did not come near this coast. Even if their ports were not so open as in other parts of the world, yet their governors, being generally Europeans who seldom remained above three years in the country, could easily be accessed so as to act very obligingly. Before leaving me, he desired me to carry his ship two or three leagues out to sea, and then to turn her adrift, on purpose to deceive the governor and the king's officers; and, if I would meet him at Hilo, about twenty-five leagues to the north-westwards, he would purchase from me any coarse goods I had to dispose of, which might be done there with all imaginable secrecy.

At this time also, the master of the small bark came off in a balsa. This is an odd sort of an embarkation, consisting of two large seal skins, separately blown up, like bladders, and made fast to pieces of wood. On this he brought two jars of brandy and forty dollars, which, considering his mean appearance, was as much as I could expect. One part of his cargo was valuable to us, a considerable quantity of excellent dried fish.

The port of Arica, formerly so famous for its great quantities of silver, is now much diminished and appears mostly a heap of ruins, except the church of St Mark, which is handsome enough, and two or three more, which still look tolerably well. In truth, Arica is now no more than a little village of about 150 families, most of them negroes, mulattoes, and Indians, with very few whites. What adds to its desolate appearance is that the houses near the sea are only constructed of crossed canes and leather thongs, or canes set on end, and covered with mats, as no rain ever falls here. So that the houses seem all in ruins when seen from the sea. The use of unburnt bricks is reserved for churches and the stateliest houses. There are also three religious houses, one a monastery of seven or eight mercenarians, a second is an hospital of the brothers of St John of God, and the third a monastery of Franciscans. Being situated on the seashore, in an open roadstead, it has no fortifications of any kind, the Spaniards thinking it sufficiently secured by the heavy surf, and the rocky bottom near the shore. These threaten inevitable destruction to any European boats, or other embarkation, except the balsas already mentioned.

Earthquakes are also frequent here. On 26 November 1705, the sea, violently agitated by an earthquake, broke down the greatest part of the town, and the ruins of its streets are to be seen at this day. What remains is not now liable to such an accident, being situated on a little rising ground at the foot of the headland. The vale of Arica is next the sea, and about three miles wide. It is barren except some parts divided into small fields of clover, some small plantations of sugar canes, with olive trees and cotton trees intermixed, and several marshes, full of the sedges of which they build their houses.

About three miles east of this, at the village of St Michael, they cultivate the *agi*, or guinea pepper. There are several detached farms exclusively devoted to this culture. In this part of the vale, very narrow, though about eighteen miles long, they yearly raise peppers to the value of above eighty thousand crowns, the Spaniards of Peru being so much addicted to this spice, that they dress no meat without it, although it is so hot and biting that no one can endure it unless accustomed to its use, and, as it cannot grow in the mountainous country around, merchants come down every year to buy these peppers, from which it is reckoned they export yearly to the value of six hundred thousand dollars, though sold cheap. It is hard to credit that such vast quantities are produced, as the country is so parched up that nothing green is to be seen. But this wonderful fertility is produced by the dung of fowls, the guano already mentioned, which is brought from Iquique, and which fertilises the soil in a wonderful manner, making it produce four or five hundred for one of all sorts of grain, as wheat, maize, and so forth, but particularly of this pepper.

They are first grown in a seedbed, for transplanting, then set out in winding lines like the letter 'S', so that they may be watered equally. They then lay about the root of each plant of guinea pepper as much guano as will lie in the hollow of the hand. When in blossom, they add a little more, and, lastly, when the pods are completely formed, an extra good handful to each plant, always taking care to supply them with water otherwise the salts contained in the manure, not being dissolved, would burn the plants, as has been found by experience.

For the carriage of this guano the people at Arica generally use that sort of little camels called llamas. The heads of these animals are small in proportion to their bodies, and are somewhat in shape between the head of a horse and that of a sheep, the upper lips being cleft like that of a hare, through which they can spit to the distance of ten paces against any one who offends them, and if the spittle happens to fall on the face of a person causes a red itchy spot. Their necks are long, and bent like that of a camel. Their ordinary height is from four to four and a half feet, and their ordinary burden does not exceed an hundredweight. They walk, holding up their heads with wonderful gravity, and at so regular a pace as no beating can quicken. At night it is impossible to make them move with their loads, for they lie down till these are taken off, then go to graze. Their ordinary food is a sort of grass called *yeho*, somewhat like a small rush, but finer, with which all the mountains are covered. They eat little, and never drink, so that they are very easily maintained. They have cloven feet like sheep, and are used at the mines to carry ore to the mills, and as soon as loaded, set off without any guide to the place where they are usually unloaded. They have a sort of spur above the foot, which renders them sure-footed among the rocks, as it serves as a kind of hook. Their hair, or wool rather, is long, white, grey, and russet, and has a strong and disagreeable scent, and though fine, is much inferior to that of the vicuña, which is shaped much like the llama, but much smaller and lighter, and with wool extraordinarily fine and much valued.

These animals are often hunted after the following manner: many Indians gather together, and drive them into some narrow pass, across which they have previously extended cords about four feet from the ground, having bits of wool or cloth hanging along them at small distances. This so frightens the vicuña they dare not pass, but gather together in a string, when the Indians kill them with stones tied to the ends of leather thongs. Should any quanacos, a larger and more

corpulent type, happen to be among the flock, these will
leap over, to be followed by all the vicuñas. There is yet
another animal of this kind, called alpagnes [alpacas],
having wool of extraordinary fineness, but their legs are
shorter, and their snouts contracted in such a manner as
to give them some resemblance to the human countenance. The Indians make several uses of these creatures
besides as beasts of burden. The wool is used to make
stuffs, cords, and sacks. Their bones are used for the con-
struction of weavers' utensils, and their dung is employed
as fuel for dressing meat, and warming their huts.

On leaving Arica, we sailed for Hilo, about seventy-
five miles to the northwest, where we arrived that same
afternoon, and saw a large ship with three small ones at
anchor. The great ship immediately hoisted French
colours, being the *Wise Solomon* of forty guns, commanded by M Dumain, whom we met at St Catherine's
Isle, and who was resolved to protect the vessels that
were beside him, and to oppose my coming into the
harbour. As it grew dark I sent my third lieutenant, Mr
La Porte, a Frenchman, to inform M Dumain who we
were, but my officer no sooner got on board than he was
tumbled out again, the Frenchman calling him a
renegado, and M Dumain sending me word he would
sink me if I attempted to anchor there. Mr La Porte told
me that, to his knowledge, French ships often accepted
Spanish commissions, when there were English cruisers
on this coast, receiving great trade privileges for this

service. He also told me he saw the French ship was double-manned and, he supposed, would come to attack me as soon as the wind was offshore. While thus talking, the French ship fired several guns at us, as if to show that they were ready and meant shortly to be with us. At first, this bravado angered me to the design of turning the *Mercury* into a fire-ship, by the help of which I might have roasted this insolent Frenchman. But, having reflected on the situation of affairs at home, and the limits of my commission, and fearing my attacking him might be deemed unjustifiable, notwithstanding his unwarranted conduct, I thought it best to leave harbour.

On 12 February 1721, half of the money taken at Arica was divided among the company according to their shares. On 22 February we found ourselves near Callao, the port of Lima. I furled all my sails, resolving to get away in the night, knowing, if we were seen, we should certainly be pursued by some Spanish men-of-war, as there are always some in that port. On 26 February 1721, the officers in the *Mercury* desired to be relieved, and I spoke to Captain Hately, whose turn it was to take the command of that bark. This gentleman had, in the past, been long a prisoner among the Spaniards in this country and, having travelled between Payta and Lima by land, had observed several rich towns, which made him conceive we might capture good prizes by cruising along the coast, as far as the island of Lobos, in latitude 7° S.

I approved of this, as it was probable they might meet some of the Panama Spanish treasure ships, which always keep well inshore to have the benefits of the land breezes.

As the company of the *Mercury* seemed delighted with this project, I augmented their complement, and allowed them a month's provisions. I also lent Captain Hately my pinnace, mounted the *Mercury* with two of our quarter-deck guns, and gave him a copy of my commission, although it was very likely we should have frequent sight of the *Mercury*, between our present intended separation, and our intended rendezvous at the island of Lobos, about 180 miles from where we then were.

With everything ready for departure, Captain Betagh (whose duty and turn it was to relieve the marine officer in the *Mercury*) being unwilling to go on, openly went among the people with a terrified countenance and told them that he and the rest that were sent to go were going to be sent to be sold and sacrificed, with a great many other expressions tending towards creating a general mutiny. I now imagined that he was about to act out what he had threatened – that it should be 'a short voyage' with me, and having prepared myself against any violence he might offer, I addressed the ship's company, telling them I could not conceive what this pestilent fellow meant by this uproar, and appealed to them if it had not been customary to relieve the officers in this manner, ever since we had taken the *Mercury?* I also asked if any ever knew me to force any man into an enterprise, rather than, on the contrary, leaving it to their own choice to go on any service out of the ship. I then desired to know who were of Betagh's opinion?

Upon this, they all declared with one voice that they had never entertained any such opinions, but, on the contrary, that I should always find them obedient to my commands. I now ordered the *Mercury* alongside, and acquainted her crew with Betagh's speech, and desired to know if any of them were apprehensive of being sold or sacrificed. At this they set up a loud 'Huzza', and a 'Hoot' at Betagh, and requested they might go on the intended cruise in the *Mercury*. Accordingly Hately and Betagh went on board that bark and put off from us, giving us three cheers before standing in for the land.

Here it may be proper to take some notice of the proceedings of the *Mercury* (which were very extra-ordinary) after she left me, as I have been informed from some of themselves, and by some prisoners, viz.: the very next day they took a small bark laden with rice, chocolate, wheat, flour, and the like, and the day following, another. On the fourth day, they took a ship of near two hundred tons worth one hundred and fifty thousand pieces of eight. Flushed with this, Betagh prevailed upon Hately, and most of the crew in the *Mercury*, not to rejoin me, saying they had now enough to appear like gentlemen as long as they lived, but would have nothing if the owners' part was taken out, and the rest divided into five hundred shares, 'And what is more,' continued he, 'we may meet the *Success* at any day, who will take all from us.' He therefore thought they ought to make their way to India, as they had sufficient provisions, and that Captain Hately was well able to navigate them to some port in the East Indies.

This plan was accepted, and they fell to leeward of the place of rendezvous. But Hately, weighing with himself the prodigious extent and possible hazards of the run across to India, and well knowing the treatment he might expect if his treachery were discovered, became irresolute, and kept hovering on the coast. In the meantime, some of his crew went away in his boat to surrender themselves to the Spanish, rather than be concerned in such a piratical undertaking.

Betagh and his accomplices kept Hately warm with liquor, and at length brought him to the resolution of leaving the South Sea. But they had no sooner clapped their helm a-weather than they saw a sail standing towards them, which proved to be a Spanish man-of-war, which spoilt their India voyage. As prisoners, the English were very indifferently used, but Betagh, being a Roman Catholic, and of a nation which the Spaniards are very fond of, Ireland, was treated with much respect, and was even made an officer. And this he certainly deserved, for he gave them the whole scheme of our voyage, and they had no doubt that I should be in their hands very speedily. And Betagh modestly desired of his new captain that when we did meet that he, Betagh, might have the honour of boarding me first.

In the morning of Monday, 29 February, we saw a vessel in the harbour of Guanchaeo, and anchored alongside her at 11am. She was called the *Carmasita*, of about one hundred tons, having only two Indian men and a boy on board, and her only loading a small quantity of timber from Guayaquil. From these prisoners, I was informed of a rich ship being in the cove of Payta (lat. 5° S), having put in to repair some gale damage. On this information I put immediately to sea, but in weighing the anchor, the cable parted, and we lost another anchor. Our prize being new, and likely to sail well, I took her with us, naming her the *St David*, intending to make her a fire-ship as soon as we should be rejoined by the *Mercury*; in which there were materials for that purpose.

Next day we looked into Cheripe, whence we chased a small vessel, which ran on shore to avoid us. The morning after, being near Lobos, our appointed rendezvous with the *Mercury*, I sent ashore my second lieutenant, Mr Randal, with two letters in separate bottles, directing Captain Hately to follow me to Payta, to which port I now made the best of my way.

On 18 March 1720, I arrived before Payta and sent Mr Randal to look into the cove, to bring an account of what ships were there. On the 21st I steered directly in for the cove, which I entered under French colours about four in the afternoon, leaving the *St David*, who had no anchors, to cruise outside. Inside we found only a small ship with timber and jerked beef, of which Mr Brooks took possession in the launch. About seven in the evening I came to anchor within three-quarters of a mile of the town, which seemed moderately large and populous, with probably some land forces for its defence, it being the rendezvous of the ships which trade between Panama and Callao. Yet, as the taking of this place was treated in our instructions as a matter of importance, I consulted with my officers as to the best manner of making the attempt. Leaving the master, Mr Coldsea, in charge, and a few hands to look after the blacks we had on board, and with orders to bring the ship nearer to the town, for the more expeditiously embarking any plunder, I landed with forty-six men about two o' clock in the morning of the 22nd, and marched directly up to the great church without the slightest opposition, for we found the town entirely deserted by the inhabitants.

At daylight, we observed large bodies of men on the hills, on both sides of the town, and expected an attack, but, on marching up towards them, they retired before us. We now took an old Indian and a boy, who told us that Captain Clipperton had been here some time before us, and had freed some prisoners ashore there. Clipperton had assured the town he meant them no injury, but that the inhabitants, not thinking fit to trust him, had removed all their valuables into the mountains, among which were four hundred thousand pieces of eight belonging to the King, which would have proved a fine prize for Clipperton, who certainly would have found no greater difficulty in taking this town than I did.

I suddenly halted, in consequence of hearing a gun fired from the ship, and soon after word was brought me that she was ashore. I hurried off as fast as I could, first planting the Union Flag in the churchyard and, as we were re-embarking, the enemy came running down the hill, hallooing after us. When I got on board, I found her entirely afloat, but within her own breadth of the rocks; however, as the water was quite smooth, we soon warped her off again.

We then returned to the town, whence the Spaniards retired as peaceably as before. The remainder of the day was employed in shipping off what plunder we could find, which consisted of hogs, brown and white *calavances*, beans, Indian corn, wheat, flour, sugar, and as many cacao, chocolate-nuts, as we were able to stow away, together with the pans and other conveniences for preparing it. So that now we were amply provided with excellent breakfast meat for the rest of our voyage, and were, besides, full of other provisions.

At eight in the morning of the 23rd, a messenger came in to know what ransom I would take for the town and the ship. I demanded ten thousand dollars in twenty-four hours. At eight next morning, I had a letter from the governor, signifying that as I wrote in French, neither he, nor any one about, him could understand its contents, but if I would write in Latin or Spanish, I might depend on a satisfactory answer. In the afternoon, in reply, I sent one of our quarterdeck guns ashore, and fired it at sunset, midnight, and break of day.

The town's messenger returned in the morning of the 25th, accompanied by the master of the ship we had taken, and on hearing of their arrival, I went on shore to know what they had to propose. I understood from them that the governor was determined not to ransom the town, and did not care what became of it, provided the churches were not burnt. Though I never had any intention to destroy any place devoted to divine worship, I answered that I should have no regard to the churches, or anything else, when I set the town on fire. I further told the master of the vessel, he might expect to see her in flames immediately, if not ransomed without delay.

This seemed to make a great impression, and he promised to return in three hours with the money. I then caused everything to be taken out of the town that could be of any use to us, after which I ordered the town to be set on fire in several places and, as the houses were old and dry, it instantly became a bonfire. In the midst of this conflagration, the *Speedwell* made many signals for me to come on board, and kept continually firing towards the mouths of the harbour. I went on board as soon as possible in a canoe, but before I reached the ship, I could distinctly see a large man-of-war with a Spanish flag at her fore-topmast head. This was the *Peregrine* (56 guns). At this sight, two of my three men were ready to faint, and if it had not been for my boatswain, I doubt if I should have got on board, and if the Spanish admiral had acted with vigour, he might have taken the ship long before I got to her.

It is bare justice to Mr Coldsea, the master, to say he fired so smartly on the Spaniard as to induce him to act with great precaution: quite unnecessary had he known our weakness. His caution, however, gave me the opportunity of getting on board. In the meantime, my officers were so unwilling to leave our gun ashore, that they spent a great while in getting it into the boat, and I was afraid the enemy would attack immediately. The Spaniard was, however, in no hurry, thinking no doubt that we could not well escape him, yet was within pistol-shot of us before the last of our men got on board.

We cut our cable, but our ship fell round the wrong way, so that I had just room enough to fall clear of the enemy. But now being close together, the formidable appearance of the enemy struck an universal damp on the spirits of my people, some of whom, in coming off from the shore, were for jumping into the water and swimming onshore, which a few actually did. As our disproportion to the *Peregrine* was so great there seemed no hopes of us escaping, as we were under his lee. I endeavoured to get into shoal water, but he becalmed me with his sails, and confined us for the best part of an hour, during which he handled us very roughly with his cannon, though making little use of his small arms. But as soon as his broadside was ready, he gave his ship the starboard helm, bringing as many of his guns to bear as possible; at the same time keeping me from the wind. We returned his fire as briskly as we could, but, in our precipitate retreat from the town, most of our small arms were wetted, so that it was long before they were of any use.

During this action, there was a strange confusion on shore, where the people had flocked down from the hills to extinguish the fire in Payta, in which some of them were busily employed, while others stood on the shore, spectators of our engagement. I was in despair of getting away from the Spaniard, unless we could somehow have an opportunity of trying our heels with him while our masts remained standing. I expected every minute that he would board us, and hearing a hallooing among them, and seeing their forecastle full of men, I concluded that they had come to this resolution, but then saw that it proceeded from our ensign being shot down, they thinking we had struck our colours. I immediately had another be displayed in the mizzen-shrouds, on sight of which they lay into us as snug as before, keeping close upon our quarter. Intending, at length, to do our business at once, they clapped their helm hard a-starboard to bring their whole broadside to bear, but their fire muzzled themselves, which gave us an opportunity to clap on a wind.

This certainly was a lucky escape, after an engagement of an hour and a half with an enemy so much our superior, for he had fifty-six guns and 450 men, while we had only twenty guns mounted and only seventy-three men, of whom eleven were negroes and two Indians. He had, further, the vast advantage of being in perfect readiness, while we were in the utmost confusion, and in the middle of the engagement, a third of my people, instead of fighting, were hard at work in preparing for an obstinate resistance, particularly the carpenter and his crew, who were busy in making portholes for stern chase guns, which, as it happened, we made no use of. Yet we were not unhurt, as the loss of my pinnace and anchor were irreparable, and may be said to have been the cause of that trouble which fell upon us soon after, as we had now only one anchor remaining, nor now did we have a small boat of any kind. I have since learnt that some of our shots in the engagement were well directed, and that we killed and wounded several of the enemy.

Having thus got away from the *Peregrine*, I slipped off again in the evening, without much ado, from the *Brilliante*, her consort, on board of which Betagh now was, and who, as I have said, *desired* to be the first to board me. We were now in a very uncomfortable situation, not having the smallest hope of meeting with the *Success*, and having learned at Payta that the Spaniards had called a halt to shipping movements, an embargo for six months, so that we had nothing to expect in the way of prizes.

Having now only one anchor and no small boat, it is not to be wondered that I gave up all idea of making an attempt on Guayaquil, which I had at first proposed, having intelligence that there were several ships of considerable value in that river, in consequence of their not sailing because of the embargo. In this situation, it was resolved, in a committee of my officers, to return to the southwards, or to windward, as the Spaniards must necessarily continue their trade with Chile, in spite of their embargo, after which, we proposed to water at Juan Fernández, and then to cruise on the coast of Conception, Valparaiso, and Coquimbo, for prizes from the coasting traders, from which we might supply ourselves with anchors, cables, and boats, and a vessel to fit out as a fire-ship.

I also proposed, before leaving the coast of Chile, to make an attempt on La Serena or Coquimbo. And after this, I proposed to proceed for the coast of Mexico, and thence to the Tres Marias and California, as the most likely means of meeting with the *Success*. Besides which, the former of these places might be commodious for taking and salting turtle, to serve as sea stores, and the latter for laying in a stock of wood and water, after which we might lie in the track of the Manila treasure ship. But if we could not succeed in that attempt, we might then satisfy ourselves with cruising for the Peruvian ships, which bring silver to Acapulco for purchasing the Indian and Chinese commodities.

My plan being approved, on 26 March 1720 we secured our masts, and fitted a new set of sails and then stood to the southward, expecting to make our passage in about five weeks. The carpenters were now set to work to build a new boat that we might have the means of rowing the casks onshore to water our ship. On 31 March, while working the pumps, the water not only came in, in greater quantity than usual, but was as black as ink, which made me suspect some water had got at our gunpowder. On going into the powder room, I found the water rushing in like a little sluice, which had already spoiled the greatest part of our powder, only six barrels remaining uninjured, which I immediately had stowed away in the bread room. We found shot had lodged in our hull, and afterwards dropped out, leaving room for a stream of water.

It pleased God that we now had fair weather, as otherwise we might have had much difficulty to keep the *Speedwell* afloat. We accordingly brought down our ship by the stern, and secured the leak effectually. At this time we had an abundant stock of provisions. Each man had a quart of chocolate and three ounces of rusk

for breakfast, and had fresh meat or fresh fish every
day for dinner, having plenty of the latter about the
ship, so that we could almost always make our choice
between dolphin and albacore. On 6 May, we made the
westernmost of the islands of Juan Fernández, otherwise called Más Afuera, or that furthest from the
mainland. The day after, our carpenters had completed
our new boat, which could carry three hogsheads of
water. On the 12th we saw the great island of Juan
Fernández (33° 40' S), a joyful sight at the time, though
not so fortunate in the sequel. We plied off and on till
the 21st, but could not get as much water on board
daily to supply our daily expenditure, owing to the
smallness of our carpenter's new boat. This made it
necessary for us to anchor in the roads while I prepared
to raft twenty tons of casks to the shore. We worked in,
and anchored in forty fathoms, carrying a warp
onshore, which we fastened to the rocks. This both
steadied the ship, and enabled us to haul our cask raft
ashore and back on board. By this means we were
ready to go to sea again next morning, having filled all
our water casks, but with variable weather had no
opportunity of so doing for four days, during which we
continued to anchor in the same manner.

25 May 1720: a hard gale came upon us from
seaward, with a great tumbling swell, by which, at
length, our cable parted. This was a dismal accident, as
we had no means whatever by which to avoid the

prospect of immediate destruction. But Providence interposed in our behalf, for had we struck only a cable's length to the east or west of where we did, we must all have inevitably perished. As it was, when our ill-fated ship touched the rock, our three masts went all away by the board, while we had all to hold fast by some part of the ship or rigging, otherwise we, too, must have all been tossed into the sea. In short, words are wanting to express the wretched condition in which we now were, or our astonishment at our unexpected and unfortunate shipwreck.

5. Residence on the island of Juan Fernández.
More factions and mutinies: I am ignored and
afraid for my life. We build a new craft, the
Recovery, and get off.

HAVING GOT ALL safe on shore, in the evening my officers
gathered around me to bear me company, and to devise
measures for procuring necessaries out of the wreck. I
would have set the people to work that very night, to
save what we could, but they were so dispersed that we
could not gather them together, and all opportunity was
lost of saving anything, except some of our firearms. So,
having lighted a fire, the officers wrapped themselves
up in what they could get, and slept very soundly,
notwithstanding the coldness of the weather, and our
hopeless situation.

In the morning, while the crew were employed in
building tents, and making other preparations, the
wreck was entirely destroyed, and every thing in her
was lost, except one cask of beef and one of *farina de
pao*, which were washed onshore. Thus all our provisions were gone, and every thing else that might
have been useful. I had saved 1,100 dollars belonging
to the owners, which happened to be in my chest in
the great cabin, all the rest of their treasure being in
the bottom of the bread room for security, and
consequently lost.

I need not say how disconsolate were my reflections on this sad accident, which had, as it were, thrown us out from the rest of the world, onto this desolate, uncultivated island, three hundred miles from the continent of Chile which was in the possession of the Spaniards, always remarkable for their ungenerous treatment of their enemies, and into whose hands we might well fall sooner or later

But I now took some pains to find out a convenient place in which to set up my tent, and at length found a commodious spot not half a mile from the sea, having a fine stream of water on each side, with trees close at hand for firing, and building our huts. The crew settled around me as well as they could, and as the cold season was coming on, some thatched their huts, while others covered them with the skins of seals and sea lions, coverings often torn off in the night by sudden flaws of wind from the mountains. Others satisfied themselves with water butts, in which they slept under cover of trees.

At first, as the weather was then too coarse for fishing, we had to live on seals, the entrails of which are tolerable food, but the constant and prodigious slaughter we made among them frightened them from our side of the island. Some of the people ate cats, which I could not bring myself to, but they declared them to be sweet nourishing food. When the weather eventually allowed us to fish, we were delivered from these hardships, in contrived wicker boats, covered with sea lions' skins, which did well enough near shore, but which durst not venture out into the bay. Consequently, we were worse provided with fish than we might otherwise have been. We fried our fish in seal oil, and ate it without bread or salt, or any other relish, except some wild sorrel.

Having thus secured ourselves from the weather, and gained a source of food, we would pass our time in the evenings around a great fire before my tent. Here my officers usually assembled; sometimes employing themselves in roasting crayfish in the embers, sometimes sinking into despondency, and at other times feeding on hopes that something might yet be done to set us again afloat. But as words were not alone sufficient I first consulted with the carpenter, who answered that he could not make bricks without straw, and then walked from me in a surly humour. From him I went to the armourer, and asked what he could that might contribute to build a small vessel. To this he answered, that he hoped he could do all the iron work, as he had fortunately saved his bellows from the wreck, with four or five *spadoes* or Spanish swords, which would afford him steel, and there was no want of iron along the shore, and doubtless other useful things. He desired therefore, that I would get some charcoal made for him, while he set up his forge.

Upon this encouragement, I called all hands, and explained to them the great probability of our being able to build a vessel sufficient to transport us from the island, but that it would be a laborious task, and would require their united best endeavours. To this they all consented, and promised to work with great diligence, begging me to give them directions how to proceed. I then ordered the men who had brought axes onshore, before the wreck, to cut wood for making charcoal, while the rest went down to the wreck to get the bowsprit ashore, of which I proposed to make the keel of our intended vessel. I prevailed on the carpenter to go with me, to fix upon the properest place for building the new vessel. The crew now found a great many useful materials about the wreck, and we laid the blocks for building upon on 8 June, with the bowsprit ready at hand to lay down as the keel.

Suddenly, the carpenter, who had been handling the work in a good temper, turned short upon me, and swore an oath that he would not do another stroke, for he would be slave to nobody, and was now on a footing with myself. This provoked me to use him somewhat roughly with my cane, but I then decided to use gentler methods and came at length to an agreement with him, to give him a four-pistole piece of money as soon as the stern and sternposts were up, and one hundred pieces of eight when the bark was finished, the money to be committed to the keeping of any one he chose to name. This being settled, he went to work upon the keel, which was to be thirty feet long, the breadth of our new ship to be sixteen feet, and her depth of hold, seven feet.

In two months we made a tolerable show, owing in a great measure to the ingenuity of Poppleston, our armourer, who never lost a minute working with his hands, or contriving in his head. He made us a small double-headed maul, hammers, chisels, and a sort of gimlets or wimbles, which performed very well. He even made a bullet-mould, and cartridge boxes fashioned from the trucks of our gun carriages, covering them with sealskins, and not only convenient, but neat. He contrived any ironwork wanted by the carpenter, and even finished a large serviceable boat, of which we stood much in need.

In the beginning of this great work the crew behaved very well, half working regularly one day, and the other half the next. They treated me with as much respect as I could wish, and even in a body thanked me for the prospect of their deliverance, while I never failed to encourage them by telling them stories of the great things that had been accomplished by the united efforts of men in similar distresses. I always pressed them to stick close to the work, that we might get our bark ready in time, and told them that, fortunately, three of the best ports in Chile were within 350 miles of us. Inspired with life and vigour, they often declared that they would exert their utmost endeavours to finish her with all expedition.

At last, however, we became a prey to faction, and I

was confirmed in the suspicion I had there was black design a-kindling. For, after completing the most laborious part of the work, they entirely neglected it, and many of my officers, deserting my society, herded with the meanest of the ship's company. And when I met any of my officers, and asked the reason of their acting so contrary to their duty, and diverting the crew from their work, some used to tell me they knew not whether they would leave the island or not, when my *bundle of sticks* was ready. And that that they cared not how matters went, for they could shift for themselves. When I spoke with the common men, some were surly, and others said they would be slaves no longer, but would do as the rest did. In the midst of these confusions, I ordered my son to hide my commission in some dry place among the woods or rocks, remembering how Captain Dampier had had his stolen in these seas.[35]

At length, one afternoon, all the crew went missing except Mr Adamson the surgeon, Mr Hendry, the agent, my son, and Mr Dodd, lieutenant of marines, who, for some reason best known to himself, was now feigning lunacy and acting the madman. I learnt that night the crew had been all day assembled at the great tree, in deep consultation, and had framed a new set of regulations and articles, by which the owners in England were excluded from any share in what we might take for the future. At the same time they divested me of all authority as captain, and regulated themselves according to the Jamaica discipline: that is, after the manner of the pirates and buccaneers of the West Indies, whereby the plunder from all prizes henceforth would be divided only among those taking them and in strict shares.

Even the chief officers had apparently concurred in the election of Morphew to be their champion and speaker. (Who else? And who, before the *Speedwell* was lost, had both made and mended their shoes.) He addressed the assembly as following:

> That they were now their own masters, and servants to none: and as Mr Shelvocke, their former captain, took upon him still to command, he ought to be informed, that whoever was now to be their commander, must be so through their courtesy. That Mr Shelvocke might have the first offer of the command, if the majority thought fit, but not otherwise. That Mr Shelvocke carried himself too lofty and arbitrarily for the command of a privateer, and ought to have continued in men-of-war, where the crew were obliged to bear all hardships quietly, whether right or wrong.

Some present, who had a regard for me, represented:

> That they had never known me treat any one unjustly or severely, and that however strict I might be, they had no one else to depend upon, and all ought to consider how many difficulties I had already brought them through. That, although they were not now in

the hands of our enemies, no one could tell how soon
others might come upon them. And, if they ever
looked to get back to England, there was no other
way but by going round the world – for which there
was no one capable of undertaking the charge
except Captain Shelvocke. They ought also to consider his commission, and the respect due to him on
that account, besides the protection that would
afford them should they happen to fall into the
hands of the Spaniards.

That is, with the privateer's commission, if taken by the
Spanish we would be treated, however so harshly, as
prisoners, but without it we would assuredly be hung
as pirates.

This remonstrance had some effect on the common
men, but they were then diverted from thoughts of
returning to obedience by no less a person than my first
lieutenant, Mr Brooks. Brooks had made Morphew his
confidant on board ship, for having served before the
mast before he was made my lieutenant, Brooks had
contracted a liking for forecastle conversation. They
were supported and encouraged by Mr Randal, my
second lieutenant, who was brother-in-law to Brooks,
and by others. The first remarkable outrage committed
by this gang of Levellers[36] was to Mr La Porte, my third
lieutenant, whom Morphew knocked down on the
beach, while Brooks stood by and witnessed this
brutality. On this being reported to me, I checked Mr

Brooks for his inhumanity, but all the answer I got was that Mr La Porte should keep a good tongue in his head and take care how he affronted anybody again, this piece of insolence serving as an introduction to what followed, which, I believe, is not to be heard of in any former expedition to these seas – or any others.

For completely running themselves down the descent of ingratitude, that night they came before my tent, and put a piece of paper in my hand which told me that as the *Speedwell* was lost, they were now at their own disposal with their obligations to the owners, and myself, having no validity, the ship being no more, and so had drawn up new articles more conducive to their own interests. First, that what money or plate was hereafter taken should be divided amongst them as quickly as possible. Secondly, that in all attacks, on land or sea, the crew's assent was to be gained. All would have single vote – the captain to have two. And declaring, as I had been their captain, I might be so still, and that they were willing to allow me six shares, as a mark of their regard, though I ought only to have four, according to what pirate captains are allotted while on Jamaica articles. In this distressed emergency, I thought it lawful, and even necessary, to submit to their demands, for if I refused it would be more than probable that if we got off this island I would be forcibly left behind or would even have had violence used on me for the sake of my commission. I therefore signed, in conjunction with the rest of my

officers, most of the whom were reduced in rank. Mr La
Porte, Mr Dodd, and Mr Hendry were declared mid-
shipmen, and as the superior officers consented to this
scheme, it could not be prevented from being carried
into execution. Mr Coldsea, the master, was the only
person who preserved a kind of neutrality, neither
promoting nor opposing their designs.

I now thought to have got them back to work on our
bark, but, instead, they demanded what little money I
had saved belonging to the owners, with which I was
obliged to comply, being 750 dollars in virgin silver, a
silver dish weighing 75 ounces, and 250 dollars in coin.
Even after this, I was treated worse than ever, the mass
of the crew being taught they were as good men as I,
and only allowing me the refuse of the fish, while
Morphew and his associates feasted on the best the sea
afforded, and wondering why I could not go out and
catch it myself. So that, in the end, I only had about me
at my table but a slender family of my surgeon, my son,
and a black who used to kill seals, go a-fishing, and get
palm cabbages in the mountains for us. They next took
the arms out of my custody, of which hitherto I had
taken great care, because, having only one flint to each
musket, and very little ammunition, I foresaw that we
would be undone if this were wasted. I represented this
to them, yet they squandered away the small remainder
of powder and bullets in killing cats, or any thing else
they could get to fire at.

This is a concise history of our transactions in the island of Juan Fernández, from 24 May to 15 August, on which day we were put into great confusion by the sight of a large ship. Before she crossed the bay, I ordered all the fires to be put out, and the negroes and Indians to be confined, lest the ship might be becalmed under the land, and any of them should attempt to swim off to her, as I conceived she might possibly be a man-of-war come to seek us, having received advice of our shipwreck. For I knew if it were discovered what we were about, we should soon have the whole force of the kingdom of Chile upon us. But our apprehensions were soon over, as the ship bore away large, and kept at too great a distance to see anything of us.

On this occasion I got most of the crew under arms, and was glad to see them in some measure obedient to command. Telling them this, I was impertinently answered that all this was for their own sakes. Before they dispersed, I represented to them the necessity of using their best endeavour to get our bark afloat, as, if discovered by the Spaniards, we might expect to be all made slaves in the mines. But the more I tried to reclaim them, the more obstinately they ran into confusion, denying everything that would do them service.

Next day there was yet another new scheme: no less than to burn our new ship, and to build two large shallops, or pinnaces, in lieu of her. Morphew and his friend Brooks were the favourers of this, aiming doubtless at a separation by this means, but, as according to their new articles everything must be determined by a majority, they assembled, with much clamour, to debate this matter in front of my tent. To put them off this ruinous plan, I represented the impracticability of building new boats, as our tools and other materials were already worn out and such a scheme could never be completed. The workmen, and a majority of the rest, sided with me, but at night the carpenter sent me word, if I did not pay him the money agreed upon at first, I should never see his face again. Wherefore, although he had not met his terms, I was obliged to raise the money for him. The most provoking part of this proposal about the boats was, that those who chiefly promoted it, were those who had never done an hour's work since we were cast away. Not gaining this point, they openly declared I should not be their captain, and should be left on the island, and that none but Brooks should command them, which was probably what that young man aspired to from the commence-ment of the mutiny, and had undoubtedly succeeded, had it not been for the people in the boatswain's tent, who refused their consent to my being left on the island: even though fond of thinking themselves their own masters, and of refusing to submit to regular command.

To complete the confusion, there arose a third party, who resolved to have nothing to do with anybody! And proposed to remain on the island. There were twelve of these, who never made their appearance except at night, when they used to come about the tents to steal powder, lead, and axes, and any thing else on which they could lay their hands. But in a little time I found means to manage them, and took from them all their arms, ammunition, axes, and other plunder, and threatened to have them treated as enemies, if they came within musket-shot of our tents.

These divisions so weakened the whole body, that they began to listen to me, and I again brought most of them into a working humour. Even Brooks came to me with a feigned submission, desiring to eat with me again, yet in the main did not lessen his esteem for Morphew one jot.

We now had the assistance of most heads and hands, but when we came to plank the bottom, we had vexatious difficulties, as our only plank consisted in pieces from the deck of our wreck, which was so dry and stubborn that fire and water had hardly any effect in making it pliable, as it rent, split, and flew in pieces like glass, so that I now began to fear that all our labour had been in vain, and we must quietly wait to be taken off by some Spanish ship, and be led off to prison. Mr Brooks was our only diver, and tried what could be recovered from that part of the wreck which had not been drifted on shore, but could only bring up one small gun, and two pieces of a large church candlestick, belonging to our owners. However, by constant labour and a variety of contrivances, we patched her up in such a manner that I dare say the like was never seen, and may safely affirm that before her, such a bottom never swam on the surface of sea.

Our small boat was launched on 9 September, and our new bark being now in a fair way of being completed, it only remained to consider what provisions we could get to support us during our voyage, all our stock being one cask of beef, five or six bushels of cassada flour, and four or five live hogs. I made several experiments to preserve both fish and seal, but found that this could not be done without salt. At length we fell upon a contrivance for curing conger eels, by splitting them, taking out their backbones, dipping them in seawater, and then drying them in a great smoke, but as no other fish could be cured in a similar manner, our fishers were directed to catch as many congers as they could.

At this time several of our people who had not hitherto done any work, began to repent of their folly, and now offered their services to go a-fishing, making idle excuses for being so long idle, asking my pardon, and promising not to lose a moment in future. They were set to make an abundance of lines of twisted ribbons, a great quantity of which had been driven onshore while the armourer supplied hooks. Then the small boat was sent to try her fortune, and returned at night with a great parcel of various kinds of fish, among which were about two hundred congers, which was a good beginning, and which were divided among the tents to be cured. The boat itself was carefully hauled onshore every night, and strictly guarded, to prevent any from stealing her, and making their escape.

By constant labour, and a variety of contrivances, we at length finished our bark, but in such a manner that I may safely assert a similar bottom never before swam on the sea. Some were employed in making twine stuff for rigging for her, patching up old canvas for sails, and a variety of other necessary contrivances, while our cooper put our casks in order, and at length we set up our masts, which were tolerably well rigged, and our bark made a decent figure. My spirits were however much damped, by the extreme difficulty of caulking her tight, as her seams were bad, our tools wretched, and our artists very indifferent. When this was done, as well we could, our bark was put into the water to try her fitness, on which there was an outcry of, 'A sieve! A sieve!'

Every one now seemed melancholy and dispirited, but in a little time, by incessant labour, we brought her into a tolerable condition. Having repaired the ship's pumps, and fitted them to the bark, the crew exclaimed that this was a poor dependence, but I exhorted them to have patience, and continue their assistance. The cooper also made a set of buckets, one for every man, to serve to bale her, in case of necessity.

Next spring-tide, which was on 5 October 1720, we

put her again into the water, naming her the *Recovery*. She answered tolerably well, and we resolved to run the hazard of going to sea in her, and made all possible dispatch in getting our things on board. Our sea-stock, besides the small quantity of beef and cassada flour formerly mentioned, consisted of 2,300 eels cured in smoke, weighing one with another about a pound each, together with about sixty gallons of seal oil, in which to fry them. Yet, after all, a dozen of our people chose to remain on shore, together with as many negroes and Indians. And so we embarked, leaving the island of Juan Fernández on the evening of 6 October 1720.

For the information of those who come later, this island enjoys a fine wholesome air, insomuch that out of seventy of us, who remained here five months and eleven days, not one among us had an hour's sickness, though we fed upon such foul diet, without bread or salt, so that we had no complaints among us, except an incessant craving appetite, and the want of our former strength and vigour. As for myself, from being corpulent, and almost crippled by the gout, I lost much of my flesh, but became one of the strongest and most active men on the island, walking much about, working hard, and never in the least afflicted with any distemper.

The soil is fertile, and abounds with many large and beautiful trees, most of them aromatic. One good property of the woods which cover this island is that they are everywhere of easy access, as there is no undergrowth, except in some of the deepest valleys, where the fern grows exceedingly high, and of which there are very large trees, with trunks of considerable solidity. Some of the English who had been formerly here, had sowed turnips, which have spread much, but my men never had patience to let any of these come to maturity. We found also plenty of watercresses and wild sorrel. Some of the hills are remarkable for a fine red earth, which I take to be the same with that of which the inhabitants of Chile make their earthenware, which is almost as beautiful as the red porcelain of China.

The northern part of the island is well watered by a great many streams which flow down narrow valleys, and we found the water to keep well at sea, as good as any in the world. Down the western peak there fall two cascades from a perpendicular height of not less than five hundred feet, close together, and about twelve feet broad. What with the rapid descent of these streams, and the numerous palm trees growing close beside them, adorned with vast clusters of red berries, the prospect is really beautiful.

We should have had no want of goats, could we have conveniently followed them in the mountains. The Spaniards left a breed of goats here, and have since endeavoured to destroy them, by leaving a breed of dogs, but without effect. Cats are also very numerous, exactly resembling our household cats in size and colour, and those of our men who eat of them, assured me they found more relief from one meal of their flesh, than from four or five of seal or fish, and, to their great satisfaction, we had a small bitch, which could catch almost any number they wanted in an hour.

There are not many sorts of birds, but the sea on the coast abounds with a greater variety of fish than almost any place I was ever in. Seals and sea lions also abound, called *lobos de la mar* by the Spaniards, 'wolves of the sea', from their resemblance to wolves. They have a fine iron-grey fur, and when full grown are as big as a large mastiff. They are naturally surly, and snarl at the approach of anyone. Instead of tails, they have two fins behind, with which they make shift to get on much faster than the sea lions, which are large unwieldy creatures, and prodigiously full of oil.

6. Proceedings in the South Sea, after leaving
Juan Fernández; conger eels our only food; a
fierce engagement. We plunder stores at Iquique;
we take the *Jesus Maria* and the town of Payta.

ONCE AT SEA, I took stock and found us to be upwards
of forty in number, crowded together, and lying on the
bundles of eels, with no means of keeping ourselves
clean, so that all our senses were offended as greatly as
possible. One conger was allowed to each man for
twenty-four hours: this creating incessant quarrels,
every one contending for the frying-pan, and our only
convenience for a fire, was a tub half filled with earth,
which made cooking so tedious, that we had the continual noise of frying from morning to night. Our water
we obtained by sucking it from the cask through a gun
barrel, used promiscuously by every one.

I proposed that we should stand for the Bay of
Conception, being the nearest which we knew. And we
were hard put to it every day, for, not having above
sixteen inches freeboard, our bark tumbled prodigiously, the water swamped over perpetually, and having
only a grating deck, and no cover but the topsail of our
bark, our pumps were barely sufficient to keep us free.

At four in the morning of the 10th, we fell in with a
large ship, and I could see by moonlight that she was
Europe-built. Our case being desperate, we stood

towards her, and were not seen until daylight. Not coming quite up with her, they began to suspect, wore ship, fired a gun, and crowded away, leaving us at a great rate. Two hours later it fell calm, when we took to our oars, and drew near her with tolerable speed. While doing so, we overhauled our small arms, which we found in bad condition, a third wanting flints. We had but three cutlasses, so that we were by no means prepared for boarding, but this would be the only means of taking the ship. We had one small cannon, which we could not mount, and were therefore obliged to fire it as it lay along the deck, while for ammunition we had only two round shot, a few chain-bolts, the clapper of the *Speedwell's* bell, and some bags of stones.

We came up with her in four hours, when I saw she had guns, big and small, and a considerable number of men, whose arms glittered in the sun. These defied us to board them, calling us 'English dogs', and at the same time gave us a volley of great and small shot, which killed our gunner, and almost cut through the foremast. This unexpected reception staggered many of my people, even the bravest, who now lay on their oars, though I urged them to keep their way. Recovering again, we rowed quite up to them, and continued to engage till all our small shot was expended, which obliged us to fall astern to make some slugs, and in this manner we made three attacks without success. That night, we were busied in making slugs, and provided a large quantity before morning, when we came to the determined resolution to boarding her, or to submit to her as prisoners.

Accordingly, at daybreak, I ordered twenty men in our yawl to lay across her bow, while I proposed to board her from the *Recovery*, but, just as we were on the point of making the attempt, a gale sprung up, and she went away from us. We learnt afterwards that she was the *Margarita*, mounting forty guns. As well as our gunner, Gilbert Henderson, being killed, three were wounded, Mr Brooks being shot through the thigh, Mr Coldsea in the groin, and one of the crew in the small of the back. Mr Coldsea lingered in a miserable condition for nine or ten months, but at length recovered. We were now in a worse condition than ever, and the sea being now rougher, I proposed to stand to the north to get into fairer weather, taking in Coquimbo in our way, to try what might be done there.

This was agreed, but the very morning in which we expected to have got into Coquimbo, a hard gale sprung up, which lasted four days, and our yawl in tow, and having only a very short rope, threatened with every sea to be thrown upon our deck. This so frightened our people, that they resolved to go ashore at the first place they could find, whereupon mentioned the island of Iquique, and the surprisal of that place, it being but a small lieutenancy, where we might get some wholesome provisions, and a better vessel. This was approved, and the sun again shining, we acquired fresh vigour, and directed our course for that island which we saw after three weeks and seemed merely a high white rock, at the foot of the high land of Carapucho.

Our small boat set off for the island about sunset, and after almost being lost among the breakers, heard the barking of dogs, and saw the light of some candles. But aware of the danger of landing in the dark, they made fast their boat to a float of weeds for want of a grapnel, and waited till daylight. They then rowed in between the rocks, welcomed on shore by some Indians. Going to the house of the lieutenant, they broke open the door, and rummaged it and the village, finding a booty more valuable to us than any gold or silver. This consisted of sixty bushels of wheat flour, 120 of beans and corn, some jerked beef, mutton, and pork, a thousandweight of well-cured fish, four or five days' eating of soft bread, and five or six jars of Peruvian wine and brandy, besides a good number of fowls and some rusk. They had also the good fortune to find a boat to bring off their plunder, which otherwise had been of little use to us, as their own boat was fully laden with men.

In the meantime, we in the *Recovery* were carried away by the current to the northward, out of sight of the island, and as they had not loaded their boats till the height of the day, they had a laborious task to row off, being very heavily laden. We, for our part, were under the melancholy apprehensions they might have deserted us, but towards evening we perceived their two boats coming fast towards us.

Words can't express our joy! The scene was now changed from famine to plenty. The loaves of soft bread were distributed, and the jars of wine broached, but I took care they should drink of it moderately, allowing each man no more than half a pint. After living a day or two on wholesome diet, we wondered how our stomachs could have digested the rank nauseous congers fried in train oil, and we could hardly believe we had lived on nothing else for a month past. I was assured by my second lieutenant, who commanded our yawl, that the Indians seemed glad of us pillaging the Spaniard, so natural is it for bad masters to find enemies in their servants.

The island of Iquique is in the latitude of 20° 45' S, about a mile from the mainland, and only about a mile and a half in circuit, the channel between it and the coast of Peru being full of rocks. It is of moderate height, and the surface consists mostly of cormorant's dung, which is so very white that places covered with it appear at a distance like chalk cliffs. It smells very offensive, yet it produces considerable gain, as several ships load here with it every year for Arica, where it is used as manure for growing capsicums. The only inhabitants of this island are negro slaves, who gather this dung into large heaps near the shore, ready for boats to take it off. The village where the lieutenant resides, and which our people plundered, is on the mainland close by the sea, and consists of about sixty scattered ill-built houses, or huts rather, and a small church. There is not the smallest verdure to be seen about it, neither does its neighbourhood afford even the smallest necessary of life, not even water, which the inhabitants have to bring in boats from the Quebrada, or breach of Pisagua, thirty miles to the north, wherefore, being so miserable a place, the advantage derived from the guano or cormorant's dung seems the only inducement for its being inhabited. To be at some distance from the excessively offensive stench of the dung, they have built their wretched habitations on the main, in a most hideous situation, and still even too near the guano, the vapours from which are even there very bad, yet not quite so suffocating as on the island. The sea here affords abundance of excellent fish, some kinds of which I had never before seen, one of them resembling a large silver eel, but much thicker in proportion. The inhabitants of this desolate and forbidding place cure these fish in a very cleanly manner, and export large quantities of them by the vessels which come for the guano.

We were informed by two Indian prisoners that the lieutenant of Iquique had a boat at Pisagua for water, which we now began to need, and I sent Mr Randal in search of her. He failed in this, but brought off a few bladders full of water, and three or four sort of floats, called balsas, composed of two large sealskins, cleverly sewed and filled with wind, and used by the fishermen for coming off and on this dangerous coast which has hardly a smooth beach from one end of it to the other.

We intended now to look into the port of Arica, but heard there was a ship there of force, so steered wide of that port for to attempt Nasca (16° S) and Pisco (13° S) – both noted for their exportation of wines and brandy. Off Nasca, two hours before daylight, we met a large ship, and though we rowed very hard, it was ten o'clock before we got up with her when they threw over a large quantity of lumber which pestered our decks. After a brisk dispute of six or seven hours, we were obliged to leave her, in consequence of the sea breeze coming in very strong. She was called the *San Francisco Palacio*, of 700 tons, eight guns, and a great number of men and small arms, but was so deeply laden that, in rolling, the water ran over her deck and out at her scuppers; indeed, she had more the appearance of an ill-contrived floating castle, than of a ship.

Thus we had the misfortune, on this forlorn voyage, to meet with the two best-equipped and armed private ships in the South Sea. This latest repulse was made a pretence for much murmuring and discontent, and some were for immediately surrendering to the enemy. To prevent this design, I ordered four men whom I thought I could trust to take the charge of our two small boats, two in each, to row from the ship so none might escape in them. But the two in the best boat deceived me and rowed for Callao where the authorities there must hear of us in a day or two. The next day I heard my first lieutenant, and Morphew, had plotted to have gone away with the other, but were hindered by the weather blowing fresh.

Next day we stood into the road of Pisco (13° 45' S), where we saw a very fine ship, and resolved immediately to board her; and to our great satisfaction, the captain and his people met us with their hats off, beseeching us to give them quarter. This vessel of about 200 tons, was called the *Jesu Maria*, laden with pitch, tar, copper, and plank, but nothing else. The captain offered sixteen thousand dollars for her ransom, but I could not comply, as the *Recovery* had disabled her masts in boarding, and also we had now a vessel in which we could at least enjoy cleanliness, to which article we had been entire strangers since our departure from Juan Fernández. We therefore made all dispatch in getting everything out of the *Recovery*.

The Spanish captain informed me that the *Margarita* had arrived some time before at Callao, where she had given a full account of her engagement with us; her captain and three men having been killed in the action, and a priest, with several others, wounded. She was now ready to put to sea again to cruise for us, with the addition of ten guns and fifty men, and that a frigate of twenty-eight guns, called the *Flying Fish*, was already out with the same intention, and that advice about us had been sent both ways along the coast, north and south, to equip what strength there was to catch us.

All night, the people of Pisco were on the alert, continually firing guns, to give us an earnest of what we were to expect if we attempted to land, but we had no such intention. Being now, as it were, in the very jaws of our enemies, next morning we gave the *Recovery* to the Spanish captain of the *Jesu Maria*, weighed, and stood out to sea, and met our own small boat with the two men who had deserted us, and who now edged down upon us, imagining we had been Spaniards. These two fellows were almost dead, having neither eaten nor drunk for three days, and had just been ashore on a small island near the harbour of Pisco, to kill some seals that they might drink their blood. Their excuse for leaving us was that they had fallen asleep, during which the breeze had wafted our bark away from them.

We proceeded along the coast cautiously, but ventured to look into the roads of Guanchaco, Malabriga, and Cheripe, where we saw no shipping, after which we passed through between the island of Lobos de Tierra and the continent, eventually standing off Payta on the evening of 25 November 1720. I first thought of a night surprise attack, even though our force was much diminished, but then thought to delay till daylight because there were so many rocks about. Besides, I thought, our vessel, being Spanish, would deceive the inhabitants.

In the morning, being observed from the shore to be tacking, the Spaniards sent off a large boat full of men to assist in bringing in our ship, and to enquire the news. Seeing this, I ordered none of our men to appear on deck but such as came nearest to Spanish complexions and dress. These would answer the questions as they might ask in hailing, and give them a rope and make them fast alongside. Others, concealed under our gunwales, with their muskets ready, would then command them into our vessel. This stratagem had its effect and I examined the prisoners as to the condition of the town, which they assured me was extremely poor, having neither money nor provisions. They showed me a small bark onshore, lately sent in by Captain Clipperton a little while before with some of his prisoners. On Clipperton's appearance everything of value in the town had apparently been removed into the country.

Yet we held on our way with Spanish colours flying, and no sooner was the anchor down I sent Mr Brooks to attack the town with twenty-four men, only the three or four who rowed appearing in view, the rest, with their arms, lying in the bottom of the boats, so that when they landed, they even found the children playing on the beach. These, on seeing armed men, took the alarm immediately, and in an instant the whole place was in confusion, all trying to escape to all points of the compass, taking no account of their wives or children, content on being too nimble to be overtaken. Some women were captured, but after being searched, had their liberty restored to them. Payta now being deserted, our party ransacked the town, but found it as poor as our prisoners reported, furnishing only a few bales of coarse cloth, about five hundredweight of dried dogfish, two or three pedlars' packs, and an inconsiderable quantity of bread and sweetmeats.

We had better fortune while at anchor, as we took a vessel that came in with fifty jars of Peruvian wine and brandy, her master having come by stealth from Callao, although orders had been given that none but ships of force should venture to sea. My people in the town were in no haste to re-embark, and when it grew dark, some of the Spaniards began to assemble, and learning that there were only eighteen English in the town, came down from the hills with great boldness. At first my crew took refuge in the largest church, but at length marched out and formed a line while beating their drum, and one of them, having fired a musket, the Spaniards hastily retreated, and our men embarked without any more alarm.

From Payta we directed our course for the island of Gorgona, in the bay of Panama, and in our passage to that place built a tank or wooden cistern in our vessel, sufficient to contain ten tons of water. On 2 December 1720 we arrived at Gorgona and had the advantage of being able to fill our water casks in the boat, the fresh water running in small streams from the rocks into the sea, and we cut our wood for fuel close to high-water mark, so that in less than forty-eight hours we completed our business, and hurried away for fear of those vessels which we understood had been sent in search of us.

Having got out of the track of the enemy's ships, we consulted as to the properest manner of proceeding – when the majority were for going directly for India. Upon this we changed the name of our vessel, from the *Jesu Maria* to the *Happy Return*, and used our best endeavours to get off from the coast of America. The winds and currents were, however, contrary, and some of our people who were adverse to this India plan did secret damage to our tank, so that the greatest part of our water leaked out. Owing to this, and our provisions being much exhausted by long delays, we were incapable of attempting so long a run. Wherefore, to procure what we wanted, I proposed making a descent on Realejo, on the coast of Mexico, (12° 28' N). In our way thither, we fell in with Cape Burica (8° N) and then, on second thoughts, I judged it might be safer to make an attempt on the island of Quibo, in latitude 7° 30' N, where, according to previous accounts, there were said to be inhabitants who lived plentifully on the produce of their island.

On 13 January 1721, then, we entered the channel between the islands of Quibo and Quivetta, in twenty fathoms water, and anchored opposite a sandy bay, which promised convenience for wooding and watering. Sending our boat to view the bay, my people reported that there was a good close harbour a little to the south, but no signs of inhabitants, except three or four huts by the shore, which they supposed had been used by pearl fishers, as there were great quantities of mother-of-pearl shells scattered about. But on consideration, I resolved not to shut up our vessel in a close harbour, for fear of bad consequences, and therefore remained at anchor in the open channel.

At daybreak next morning, we saw two piraguas, or large boats, under Spanish colours, rowing in for Quivetta. This gave me apprehension they had some intelligence of us, and intended an attack. The mulattoes on the coast of Mexico are remarkable for their courage, and have sometimes done very bold actions, even in such paltry vessels as these we now saw. These, however, steered into a small cove on Quivetta, which satisfied me they had no intentions upon us.

I now sent Mr Brooks in our yawl to attack them, when they were all ashore and he did so and brought away their two boats, and a negro and a mulatto, the rest taking refuge in the woods. We took their provisions, a small quantity of pork, with plantains, some green, some ripe, and some dried, but were then mortified by the mulatto telling us that a vessel laden with provisions had passed very close in the night. He also promised to bring us to a place where we might supply ourselves without hazard, wherefore we made all possible dispatch in getting in wood and water.

We weighed on 16 January 1721, steering for Mariato, the westernmost point of the gulf of St Martin. In going out from the channel of Quibo, we were in imminent danger of being forced by the current upon two rocks at a small distance from each other, but having cleared them, we steered through Canal Bueno, or the good channel, or straits, being free from rocks or shoals.

At the south entrance of these straits, at the distance of a league from point Mariato, is the island of Cebaco, in my opinion about thirty miles in circumference. I ran along the south end of that island, and in the evening of 19 January got safe in between it and point Mariato, and anchored in six fathoms, over against a green field, being the only clear spot thereabout. Our pilot advised us to land about three hours before day, when we should be in good time for the plantations. Accordingly, I went at two in the morning in our own small boat, the two lieutenants being in the two piraguas, and left my son with a few hands to take care of the ship.

Our pilot carried us a little up the river of St Martin, and then through several branches or narrow creeks, with overhanging trees, so we hardly had room to row. Not liking this, I kept a watchful eye on our guide, suspecting no good design in his head. We landed just at daybreak, in a fine plain, or savannah, and, after a march of three miles, came to two farmhouses, whence the inhabitants made their escape, except the wife and children belonging to one of them. We had the satisfaction of seeing that this place answered the description given by our guide, being surrounded by numerous flocks of black cattle, with plenty of hogs and fowl, together with dried beef, plantains, and maize, and, in the mean time, we had a breakfast of hot cakes and milk.

When it was broad day, I saw our ship close by us, on which I asked our guide, why he had brought us so far about? He said there was a river between us and the shore, and he was not sure if it were fordable. I therefore sent some to try, who found it only knee deep, on which, to avoid carrying our plunder so far by land, I ordered our boats to leave the river of St Martin, and to row to the beach over against the ship. We had not been long at the farmhouse till the master of the family came to us, bringing several horses with him, and offering to serve us as far as he could. This offer we kindly accepted, and we employed him to carry all we thought fit to our boats. He then went among his black cattle, and brought us as many as we thought we could cure.

We brought them back to the ship, but as we had but little salt, and not the water to keep them alive at sea, we killed them as soon as they came on board. We preserved them by cutting their flesh into long slips, about a finger's thickness, and then sprinkled them with a small quantity of salt, using about four or five pounds to the hundredweight. After lying two or three hours in the salt, we hung them up to dry in the sun for two or three days, which were then perfectly cured, much better than could have been done by any quantity of the best salt. Having thus procured all we proposed at this place, we departed next morning, our decks full of fowls and hogs, among the latter of which was one having its navel on its back, and called a peccary. The Spaniards say that this animal, although but small even at its full growth, is a terrible creature to meet wild in the woods.

Returning through the Canal Bueno, we stopped at Quibo to complete our water, and on leaving that island, gave the largest piragua to our two prisoners.

7. Drink puts me again in fear of my life. We meet with Captain Clipperton and the *Success*. I go on board to find him suspicious of me; next morning he slips away. I wish to go on cruising, but the crew desire India. Almost starving, we are forced to eat the congers now rotting for months in the bilges.

THE WINE AND BRANDY we had lately taken in prizes had the effect of dividing my ship's company into two parties. Those who were formerly firmly united, now being inveterate enemies, insomuch as within the space of one night, each of the ringleaders of both came to warn me the other had a design on my life, and urging me to murder those of the opposite faction. It is to be wondered how some great evil was diverted, as I could use no other means than calm advice, while it was utterly out of my power to prevent them getting drunk as often as they pleased, in which condition they would fall to fighting, while I, more than once, had my clothes almost torn off my back endeavouring to part them. Happily, the liquor did not last long, but while it did I found it was unsafe to lay my head on my pillow, and was almost wearied out of my life.

My land, as well as sea, officers, were now obliged to learn to steer, and to take their turns at the helm, such being the pass to which they had brought themselves by destroying my authority, and thereby losing their own. The crew, however, still had recourse to me at all emergencies, obeying me punctually while these lasted, and abusing me plentifully when they were over.

On 25 January 1721, a sail was raised in the morning, about two leagues to leeward, and we gave chase. But seeing she was Europe-built, and fearing she might be a man-of-war belonging to the enemy, I hauled on a wind, and in half an hour it fell dead calm. We soon after saw a boat rowing towards us from this vessel, which proved the pinnace of our consort the *Success*, commanded by her first lieutenant, Mr Davidson. This was a most unexpected meeting. He was surprised to find me in so mean a condition; I no less surprised so to find him in these seas. I gave him an account of our misfortunes, and he related all the remarkable incidents that had befallen them.

A breeze springing up, I bore down upon the *Success*, and went aboard. Here I gave Captain Clipperton, and Mr Godfrey, the owners' agent-general, the whole history of my voyage, expecting, in return, to be treated as one belonging to the same interest. Instead, I found them unwilling to have anything to do with me, now that my ship was lost. I trusted, however, that Captain Clipperton would let me have such necessaries as he could spare, on which he said, I should know more of his mind next day. Among other discourses, he told me that he was just come from the island of Cocos, his crew very ill, and on short allowance. I then offered to pilot him to Mariato, where he might have refreshed his company, and supplied his wants, but he was resolved to make best of way for the Tres Marias, where, he said, there was plenty of turtle to be had, and so I left him for the night.

Next morning, sailing across to go on board again with some of my officers, Captain Clipperton spread all his canvas, and crowded away from us. I returned to my ship, fired several guns, and made signals of distress, which were not heeded, till his officers exclaimed against his barbarity, and at last he brought to. Coming up with him again, I sent Mr Brooks to know the reason of his abrupt departure, and to request the supply of several necessaries, which I said I would pay for. On these terms, he spared me two quarterdeck guns, sixty round shot, some musket balls and flints, a Spanish chart of the coast of Mexico, with part of China and India, a half-hour glass and half-minute glass, a compass, and about three hundredweight of salt. But all my arguments could not prevail with him to let me have any thing out of his medicine chest for Mr Coldsea, who was still very ill of his wound. For what we did have, we returned some bales of coarse broadcloth, as much pitch and tar as he desired, and some pigs of copper; I gave him also a large silver ladle in return for a dozen Spanish swords.

After this, I offered my services, assuring him I had

a pretty good ship, and that our cargo was of some value. To this he answered: if my cargo were gold, he had no business with me, and I must take care of myself. Mr Hendry, our agent, Mr Rainor, and Mr Dodd, our lieutenant of marines, seeing but little prospect we should ever get home, and weary of the hard work they claimed imposed upon them, desired to go on board the *Success* for a passage to England, which I consented to, and Captain Clipperton then left us to shift for ourselves. I was now for returning southwards, to try our fortunes in the bay of Panama, but the majority opposed me through fear, insisting on going to the Tres Marias, for turtle, and then to stretch over for India. We accordingly directed our course that way, but as the wind near the land continued in the west, and the coast of Mexico trended nearly northwest by west we crept so slowly that we began to be very short of provisions. We tried again for Realijo, but were frustrated, being blown past by a *tequante peque*, for so the Spaniards on this coast call a violent gale at northeast. As we continued our voyage along shore, we again fell in with the *Success*, then in quest of the town of Sansonate, expecting there to receive the ransom of the Marquis of Villa Rocha who had been some time a prisoner on board. We ranged close under her stern, and asked how Captain Clipperton and the rest of the gentlemen did, but received no answer, and the *Success* steered one way, while we went another.

After this, calms, contrary winds, and unaccountable currents reduced us to a very short food allowance, which we were forced to diminish daily, and would have known great distress, had we not from time to time found turtle floating on the surface of the sea, discovering them even at great distances, by the seabirds perching on their backs. But a sight of these often forced us to forgo taking advantage of a wind, and they had a still a worse effect, as dressing them occasioned a great consumption of our water. Being now threatened with almost certain perdition if means were not fallen upon to avoid a state of absolute famine, I proposed that we should attempt to plunder some small town along the shore. Guatalco was the nearest port but, as we were standing in for it, we saw a sail a considerable way to leeward, which we considered more proper for us and so bore down upon her, which proved again to be the *Success*. When sufficiently near, I made the private signal but Captain Clipperton hauled his wind, and did not lie by a moment for us to get up with him.

We were now so far to leeward of Guatalco, that it was in vain to beat up for that port, especially on an uncertainty. We were now reduced to such a small daily allowance of calavances, barely sufficient to keep us alive, and so had to recourse to the remainder of our smoked congers which had been soaking and rotting in the bilgewater for some months, and were now as disgusting food as any could be. Under these calamitous circumstances, we again met the *Success*, and having exchanged signals, we stood so near that a biscuit might have been thrown aboard. Yet we did not exchange a word as Clipperton had ordered his officers and ship's company to ignore us. Yet though he would not assist us, Captain Clipperton was so aware of the hazards we would face if we tried for India, that he said the child just born would be grey-haired before we should arrive there.

In this most miserable situation, wandering upon an inhospitable coast in extremes, and in want of every thing, on 12 March, off the port of Acapulco towards evening, we saw a ship between us and the shore, again the *Success*, but now Clipperton not only answered my private signal, but also that for speaking with me. After his late inhumane behaviour, I would hardly have trusted him, had we not been so near Acapulco, where I thought he meant to cruise for the Manila treasure ships, and now wished to have our assistance. Therefore I bore down alongside. He sent across his second lieutenant, Captain Cook, with a very obliging letter, telling me he was cruising for the homeward-bound Manila ships, and desiring me to assist; that I should come aboard next morning, to form the best plan of attacking her, and he proposed an union of the two ships' companies. I was well pleased at this, and returned answer I should be with him early. I then read his letter to the crew, who all expressed their readiness to join the enterprise but, as Clipperton had used us so unhandsomely, desired me to have some security for their shares, signed by Clipperton, Godfrey, the owners' agent, and the rest of the officers in the *Success*.

I went aboard the next morning, accompanied by Brooks and Randal, my lieutenants. I was received with much apparent civility, all animosities seemingly forgotten. I first told Captain Clipperton and Mr Godfrey of the paper requested by my officers and men, entitling them to such shares as were allowed by the original articles. To this they readily consented, and drew up a document fully answerable to my people's desires. We then agreed that I should send most of my people on board the *Success* as soon as the Manila ship appeared, leaving only a small boat's crew with me to bring me away in case I should need to use the *Speedwell* as a fire-ship, should the Manila ship should prove too hard for the *Success*. We also determined to board her at once, as otherwise we should have much the worst of the contest, owing to her superior weight of guns, and her better ability to bear a cannonade. Clipperton assured me that ship was to sail from Acapulco within a day or two after Passion week, a fortnight hence.

Before returning to the *Speedwell*, I informed Captain Clipperton of our scarcity of water. He told me he had eighty tons, and would spare me as much as I wanted, or anything else. I informed my crew of what had passed on the *Success*, and now had the pleasure of enjoying my command as fully as ever, as my whole remaining crew, from the highest to the lowest, expressed their satisfaction at our present prospects. Morphew, the ringleader of all our disorders, fearing my future resentments, contrived now to insinuate himself into the favour of Captain Clipperton and his officers by a submissive deportment, and presents and, in the end, left me on 14 March for the *Success*.

On 15 March Mr Rainor came on board my ship to visit his old shipmates, and stayed all night. I constantly reminded Clipperton of our want of water, and he as often promised to supply us with a large quantity at once. We thus continued to cruise in good order, and with great hopes, till the 17th, when I had to suffer the most prodigious and perfidious piece of treachery imaginable, which happened thus.

By day we would cruise off and on the shore, at a convenient distance, so as not to be discovered, but near enough that it was impossible for any ship to leave Acapulco without being seen by us. As my ship did not sail so well as the *Success*, Clipperton would shorten sail at nights, but showing us all the necessary lights. Towards evening of that day, 27 March 1721, he moved about six miles ahead of us, but lowering no sail for us to come up with him. I kept after him however, till almost ashore on the breakers, when I had to tack and stand out to sea. Next morning no *Success* was to be seen, which reduced us to the most terrible apprehensions, considering our situation for want of water, and our vast distance from any place where we could expect to procure any. We had now no other choice but either to beat up 650 miles for the Tres Marias, or to bear away for the gulf of Amapala, at a much greater distance.

I was later informed by some of Clipperton's officers, whom I met in China, that he had done this cruel action absolutely against their repeated remonstrances, who abhorred such an act of barbarity. I also learnt afterwards, by some Spaniards from Manila, that the Acapulco ship sailed about a week after we desisted from cruising for her. This ship was the *Santo Christo*, carrying upwards of forty brass guns, and exceedingly rich. In the situation we were now reduced to, under terrible inconveniences, distressed for water and provisions, and weak in point of number, everything was to be hazarded and any experiment tried. Yet so far from being united by our common danger, our people could not be restrained even within the bounds of common civility.

Winds and weather being favourable, we found ourselves before the port of Aeazualte, on the river Sansonate on 30 March, about sunset, when we discovered a ship of good size at anchor in the harbour. Being a fine moonlight evening, I sent my first lieutenant in the yawl, with some of our best hands, to see what she was. Soon afterwards we heard some guns fired, and the lieutenant returned to report a stout ship, having at least one tier of guns. Little regarding her apparent strength or our own weakness, as necessities made us a match for her, we continued plying in all night, and prepared to engage her. At sunrise the land breeze blew so fresh from the shore, that we worked in but slowly, and in the meantime we received all their fire on but without returning a single shot.

Their small boat was employed in bringing off soldiers from the shore to reinforce them, and they hung up jars containing about ten gallons of gunpowder, with fuses, at each main and fore-yardarm, and at the bowsprit, to let fall on our deck should we come alongside to board them, which contrivances would have destroyed both ships, and all in them. So desperate preparations bespoke a warm reception, but as our case would not admit of delay, about eleven in the forenoon the sea breeze set in and, running in, I ordered all our three guns to be placed on that side from which we were likely to engage. As we ran faster towards them, our small arms were effectually employed to break their powder jars before we should board them, which we did, and grappling alongside of her, they submitted after exchanging a few shots.

This ship was named the *Sacra Familia*, of 300 tons, six guns, and seventy men, having a great many small arms, shot, and hand grenades. She had arrived some time before from Callao, with wine and brandy, but had now nothing on board except fifty jars of gunpowder, a small quantity of rusk, and some jerked beef. So while she was hardly worth the risk and trouble of the capture, she had the character of sailing better, and was much better fitted than our ship. I resolved to exchange, and we went aboard the prize, which we learned had been fitted out and commissioned for the express purpose of taking us. To do justice to my people, our small arms were handled with much dexterity on this occasion, but, having been chiefly directed at the powder jars, the only person killed was their boatswain, with one slightly wounded. On our side, no damage was sustained. A merchant, made prisoner at this time, seemed inclined to purchase our old ship, the *Jesu Maria*, and hearing her cargo consisted of pitch, tar, and copper, he consented to my ransom demands, and I allowed him ashore to raise the agreed sum.

We had so few provisions that we could not afford to keep any prisoners, and therefore dismissed all the whites, Indians, and others, except some negroes whom we detained to assist in working the ship and, that we might lose as little time as possible, we set immediately to overhauling sails and rigging to get our new ship ready for sea. While thus employed, I received a letter from the governor of the place, which none of us could understand, but learnt by the messenger that there might be a truce concluded between the crowns of Britain and Spain, and that the governor wanted me to stay on five days, that he might satisfy me of this.

I thought this odd, asking the messenger why the governor had not rather sent me a flag of truce in the morning instead of boatloads of soldiers to sink me? And saying also, if this story were true, we ought to have found the alleged intelligence on the *Sacra Familia*, and likewise extraordinary, that none of the officers in the prize should know any thing of the matter, yet I had so great a regard for even the name of peace that I would wait fifteen days, if the governor would supply us with provisions and water. Otherwise I would not consent to stay twenty-four hours. I sent also a short written answer to the governor, excusing our imperfect knowledge of the Spanish language and stating that if peace were actually concluded between our sovereigns, that I was ready to act as he desired, but on due proof. And that I hoped, as we were now friends, that he would allow us water and provisions. On receipt of this, the governor expressed great satisfaction, and seemed to make no difficulties. Our boats went ashore every morning, under a flag of truce, and we received for the first four days eight small jars of water daily. On the fifth day they reduced us to five jars, and during the whole time only one small cow was sent us.

Then a boat came off full of men, among whom were two priests, who brought with them a paper in Spanish, which they called the 'Articles of Peace', but it was so wretchedly written and blotted, we should have hard puzzled to read it, had it even been in English. I therefore desired the priests to translate it into Latin, which they promised to do, taking it back with them for that purpose. They also remarked that the governor meant to send for some Englishmen from Guatemala, if I would continue there three days longer. To this I replied he might take his own time. Two days after, our boat going ashore as usual, the governor ordered her and her crew to be seized. I was all day in suspense, not imagining the governor would make such a breach of the law of nations. In the evening, two of the boat's crew came off in an old leaky canoe, bringing a letter from the governor, and another from Mr Brooks, my first lieutenant, and now one of the prisoners. The governor required me to deliver up the *Sacra Familia* and also that we should all surrender, otherwise he would declare us pirates. Mr Brooks' letter told me he believed the governor meant to bully me.

The governor proposed two ways for conveying us from the Spanish dominions, one of which was by Vera Cruz overland, and the other by sea to Lima. But I liked neither of these, not choosing a journey of 1,300 miles at least, through a country inhabited by a barbarous people, nor yet a voyage to Lima under their promise of safe conduct. My two men told me that one of the other crewmen, Frederick Mackenzie, had let the governor into the secret of our necessities, and our great need of water, and he believed he now had us safe enough. I now sent a letter in French to the governor offering, if I could be assured of a safe conduct for ourselves and effects, to go via Panama, and thence by way of Portobello, to one of the British colonies. I also told him that if he desired to treat on this, he might fire two guns, and send off my other people with the usual supply of water, otherwise necessity would compel us to sail that night. Receiving no reply, I weighed before daybreak next morning, 7 April 1721, and made sail, having only five days water on board, leaving the *Jesu Maria* behind, a much more valuable ship than the one I took away.

8. I consider surrendering at Panama. We suffer extreme thirst, drinking urine and seawater, but are saved by making the isle of Cano.

ON GOING TO SEA, we reduced ourselves to one pint of water in twenty-four hours, and directed our course for the gulf of Amapala, about 126 miles east-southeast, meaning to water on the island of Tigers. The loss of my officer and boat's crew, unfortunately left behind, so lessened our strength that we should never have been able to manage this great ship with her heavy cotton sails, but for our negro prisoners, who proved to be very good sailors. As the loss of our small boat was a great inconvenience for casking-off water, I meant only to stow enough to take us to Panama, where we were determined to surrender ourselves, if it were really peace. I thought we might contrive to get such a quantity of water as might suffice, in two or three days by means of our canoe. The winds being favourable, we reached the Gulf of Amapala in ten days, but we could find no water.

Surrounded on all sides with difficulties, we weighed again on 13 April, when I brought our people to a resolution not to surrender on any account, let the consequence be what it might. We had not now forty gallons of water in the ship, and no other liquids, and now came to an allowance of half a pint each every twenty-four hours, even this being too large, considering we could get none nearer than the island of Quibo, which was about 480 miles from the gulf of Amapala, while we on board were forty-three in number, including our negroes. We were thirteen days on this allowance as we steered for Quibo, with uncertain winds and weather, always wishing for rain and expecting it from many louring black clouds which seemed every minute ready to discharge their burdens, yet never did it rain to any purpose. No one who has not experienced it can conceive our perpetual extremity of thirst in such sultry heat, which would not permit us to eat an ounce of victuals in a day. We even drank our urine, which moistened our mouths indeed, but excited our thirst the more. Some even drank large draughts of seawater, which had like to have killed them.

On 25 April 1721, we came to the island of Cano, in latitude 8° 47' N which, by the verdure, promised to yield us water if our canoe could get on shore. In this hope we came to anchor off the island, and it was as much as we could do to furl our sails, secure our cable, and execute the other necessary labours, so ill and exhausted were we. We imagined we could see a run of water, yet dreaded the dangerous surf which seemed to break all round the island. Mr Randal was sent in with the small boat and some jars to try what could be done, but not appearing by late at night, I became apprehensive he was lost. At length he came back, with his jars filled, and any one may guess our unspeakable joy on being thus delivered from the jaws of death. He did not bring above sixty or seventy gallons, and I was at great pains to restrain my men from using it immoderately, allowing only a quart immediately to each man. What made me the more strict on this occasion was that Mr Randal assured me we should hardly get any more, the breakers round the island being so very dangerous.

That very night we chanced to have a shower of rain, to catch which we used every expedient: sheets, blankets, and sails. Next day I sent our boatswain to make another try ashore, but after going round the whole island, wasting the entire day in search of a smooth beach, he could not see a single spot where he might venture on shore. But thinking we had a sufficient stock to carry us to Quibo, we weighed next day, and while ranging near the island, this time saw a landing place, on which I sent our canoe again, which brought back nine jars of water.

Pursuing our course to the southeast we arrived in a few days at Quibo (8° N), anchoring at the same place where we had been formerly. We wooded and watered at this island with tolerable cheerfulness, yet without any great hurry, chiefly because we were now within 180 miles of Panama, and it was requisite for us to deliberate very seriously on whether or not to surrender to the Spaniard. We considered Panama a good place to treat on this subject, as not being any way strong towards the sea, and as we had a good ship, it would be

no difficult matter to settle the terms of our surrender
before giving ourselves into their hands. We also
reckoned on some assistance from officials of the South
Sea Company, resident there, who, if a peace were
actually concluded in Europe, might intercede for us,
and procure us a passage home.

Yet as there was something extremely disagreeable in
the idea of a surrender, especially to such as the
Spaniards, we were in no great hurry, particularly as we
were now somewhat at ease, enjoying many conveniences to which we had long been strangers. The free
use we made of the excellent fruits growing on this
island brought the flux among us, which weakened us
very much, and interrupted our work for some days, yet
in the main did us little hurt, or rather tended to
preserve us from the scurvy. We deliberated and consulted as to our future conduct, but our views were so
discordant, and our minds so distracted, that we could
come to no resolution except that of continuing here, in
hopes of something happening to our advantage. But
eventually decided to stand out for Panama, and did so,
leaving behind us the isle of Quibo.

The island itself is about twenty-four English miles
from north to south, and twelve from east to west. It is
of moderate height, covered all over with inaccessible
woods, always green, and, though uninhabited, abounds
with papaws and limes, and some other fruits I never
saw before. The pearl fishers, not being able to follow

their occupation during the vandevals, or black stormy months, from the beginning of June to the end of November, have a few scattered huts used during their season, in which they sleep and open their oysters, so that the sandy beach is covered with fine mother-of-pearl shells. By wading, we could reach down for large pearl oysters with our hands, but found them as tough as leather, and quite unpalatable. We occasionally observed a large kind of flat fish, which often sprung a great way out of the water, and which are said to be very destructive to the divers; for, when divers return to the surface, these fish may wrap themselves round the diver, and hold them fast till drowned. To guard against this, the divers always carry a sharp-pointed knife, and on seeing any of these fish above them, present the point over their heads, and stick it into the fish's belly. The divers are also subject to great danger from alligators, which swarm in this part of the sea; and we fancied we saw one swimming below the surface near Mariato Point, only a few leagues from hence.

This island also has a great variety of birds, of black monkeys and of iguanas, which last mostly frequent the streams of fresh water. Some of these iguanas are of extraordinary size, being of a grey colour with black streaks, those about the head being brown. Quibo is also a most convenient place for procuring wood and water, as the wood grows in abundance within twenty yards of the sea, and there are several streams of fresh water crossing the beach.

Having got clear of this place, and thinking of nothing but our speedy return to Europe by surrendering at Panama, we met with strong adverse currents, until on 15 May, a small bark called the *Holy Sacrament* bore down upon us, mistaking us for Spaniards. She was from Cheriqui, and laden with dried beef, pork, and live hogs. We took her; and her master, though much surprised at first, soon recovered on being told we were bound for Panama, and readily offered to pilot us thither, being bound himself for that port. He had heard no news of any peace or truce between Britain and Spain. He also begged us to take him in tow, as his vessel was almost sunk through leaks, his people too exhausted to stand to the pumps, and his hogs almost dead for want of water. I obliged him in this, sending some of my people to assist in the pumping the bark, and even spared some water and maize for the hogs.

I was rejoiced at this bark having fallen into our hands; because, if there were no truce and the story of the governor of Sansonate false, we might be thoroughly enabled to go to India, with the provisions found on this bark. At the same time, every one of us was so worn out by a continual want, and so disheartened by perpetual misfortunes, that we were tired of the sea, and willing to embrace any opportunity of getting ashore. It would be essential to discover the state of affairs between England and Spain. To ascertain this, I would anchor a great way short of Panama, sending someone ashore with a flag of truce to attempt to agree to safe and honourable terms with the president, while still keeping out of his hands. After a while, however, we still had not determined who should be the bearer of the flag of truce; for there was a fear among my people, after so much treachery, that the messenger might only make terms for himself, and not return again; wherefore, my son was chosen, his return being assured for my sake.

On 17 May, another bark approached, but after coming pretty near, sheared off. At this, I sent Mr Randal in our canoe, to inform them of our design, but they hoisted Spanish colours on his approach, and fired on him. Next morning, we looked into the bay, and found her at anchor, but she renewed her fire on our approach. At his own request, I now sent the master of the *Holy Sacrament* in a canoe, with four negroes and a flag of truce, to inform the people in the other bark of our intentions. A gale of wind interrupted this plan, by forcing the canoe onshore, I dare say without danger, as they seemed to land by choice.

On 19 May we saw a sail ahead of us standing along shore, on which we let go the *Holy Sacrament*, in which there were four of our own people as the prize crew, and five Spaniards. By spreading all the sail we could, by night we were at a considerable distance from the *Holy Sacrament* and I was for lying-to, that she might come up with us. But the majority insisted we should crowd on sail in chase, so that by daybreak of the 20th we were within less than gunshot of the stranger. I immediately hoisted our colours, fired a gun to leeward, and sent a man to wave a white flag on our poop, in a token of truce. But they continually fired at us, having their decks full of men, who kept hallooing and abusing us with the grossest epithets: '*borachos*' and '*peros Ingleses*', or 'drunkards' and 'English dogs'. Still I made no return, but came close on their quarter, and then sent one of their countrymen to our bowsprit end, to inform them we were bound for Panama, and wished to treat.

Their reply was to continuing their fire, whilst still calling us *borachos* and *peros Ingleses* and other gross appellations and vile threatenings until, at length, tired of their presumptions, I thought it time to begin with them. I therefore met them with the helm, giving them so warm a reception that they soon sheered off. We just missed catching hold of them, and as it fell calm, we continued to engage her for two or three hours at the distance of musket shot. A breeze at length sprung up, when we neared them, and their courage subsided in proportion as we approached. Their captain still encouraged them to fight, bravely exposing himself in an open manner, till he was at length shot through the body, and dropped down dead, on which they immediately called out for quarter, and thus ended the dispute.

We commanded them to hoist out their launch, but they answered that their tackle and rigging were so

shattered that they could not comply, wherefore I sent
Mr Randal and two or three more in our canoe, who
found all her people most submissively asking for
mercy. Mr Randal sent the most considerable of the
prisoners on board my ship, who informed me their
vessel was *La Conception de Recova*, 200 tons burden
belonging to Callao, but last from Guanchaco, and
laden with flour, loaves of sugar, boxes of marmalade,
and jars of preserved peaches, grapes, limes, and such
like. She mounted six guns, and carried above seventy
men, another that had been fitted out and commissioned purposely to take us. On their side, in this
engagement, the Spanish captain and one negro were
killed, and one or two slightly wounded, but their
masts, sails, and rigging were much shattered. On our
part, the gunner only was slightly wounded, and a small
piece was carried out of the side of our mainmast.

We had now above eighty prisoners of all sorts, and
only twenty-six of ourselves. When the Spanish gentlemen came on board, they immediately laid the whole
blame for not treating with us on their dead captain,
Don Joseph Desorio, who vowed he would listen to no
terms but his own, and was resolved to take us by force.
There were several persons of note among our prisoners,
particularly Don Baltazzar de Abarca, Conde de la
Rosa, a European nobleman, who had been governor of
Pisco on the coast of Peru, and was now on his return
for Spain, a Captain Morel who had been formerly

taken by Captain Rogers, and several others. We treated them all with the utmost civility, at which they wondered because, from their own prejudices and harsh behaviour towards their prisoners, they expected us to deal with them very roughly.

In the situation where we now lay, we were in the track of all the ships bound for Panama, not above thirty miles from that place, our numbers being very few, and even part of our crew sick. For these reasons, as expeditiously as possible we removed the contents of our new prize into our own ship and, though the far greater part of the work was done by our prisoners, it took us full two days. Owing to this, and faint winds and calms, we did not rejoin the *Holy Sacrament* till 22 May. As we bore down towards her, we were astonished to see her broach to, then fall off again, although all her sails were set and, what amazed us more, could not see any person on her deck.

I sent a small boat over, and the officer immediately called that there was not a man on board, but that her decks were covered with blood. By this, it seemed evident that the Spaniards had overpowered and murdered my four men, doubtless taking them in their sleep. Yet it is probable the murderers lost their own lives, for being eighty miles from land, and having no boat, they probably jumped into the sea on the reappearance of our ship, to try to swim ashore, and no doubt met the death they so justly merited. This tragical affair spoiled the satisfaction on account of our prize, and raised an universal melancholy among us.

On seeing this sudden change, our prisoners now became fearful we might revenge on them the fate of our unhappy companions. I, on my side, became alarmed lest their apprehensions might stir them up to some desperate attempt on us, they being eighty in number, we at this time having no more than seventeen on board, and when altogether only twenty-five that could stand on their legs. I was therefore compelled to appear somewhat stern in ordering all our prisoners into the gallery, except the nobleman and a few of the chiefs, who were kept under strict guard in the great cabin. These Spanish gentlemen lamented the murder of our men, and their own hard fate, and let fall some expressions, by which I perceived they were afraid I meant to show some severities to their own crew.

Having a good interpreter, I assured them I was not of a revengeful disposition, and besides, that the laws of my country would restrain me if I were, as I acted by my king's commission, whose orders strictly forbid all acts of inhumanity or oppression towards prisoners, on which assurances they might rest satisfied of their safety. In reply, they begged me to think myself secure, as on their honour that they would make no attempt against us, and could never make sufficient return for the generous treatment I had given them. Notwith-standing this declaration, I took measures to secure our numerous prisoners of the meaner sort. For after taking out of the *Holy Sacrament* all her jerked beef that remained fit for use, I placed them in that vessel, under the command of officers of the *Conception*. Next day, being as willing to get rid of them as they were to get back their own ship, I took every thing out of the *Conception* that could be of use to us, sufficient for twelve months' provisions of bread, flour, sugar, and sweetmeats, both for ourselves and the *Success*, which we expected to meet with at the Tres Marias, being a stranger then to Clipperton's faithless desertion.

I took also away her launch and negroes, the latter to assist us in working our ship, the *Holy Sacrament*, now not having sufficient strength among ourselves for a run to the East Indies seeing we had a large ship and seventy-five degrees of longitude to sail. I thought we could do no other than reinforce ourselves by the assistance of these blacks, who are commonly good sailors; and indeed, as it afterwards happened, we should never have reached the coasts of Asia, or any other land, without them. I then delivered up the *Conception* back to the Spanish, which was not only an act of generosity to our prisoners, but an act of prudence with regard to ourselves.

The next great point to be managed, was to get my crew to consent to sail so far north as California, previous to our intended voyage to the East Indies, for which we were not in so good a condition as we could wish, though much better than before, everything considered. For we now had a good ship, with fifteen guns and sufficient ammunition, together with a reasonable quantity of provisions, but we still wanted to complete our wood and water for so long a voyage, the procuring of which was to be our first care.

The ship's company were for going to Quibo for this purpose, as nearest us, but that place had two great inconveniences. The first was the danger of the harbour, as the stormy season was coming on, and we were but indifferently provided with ground tackle. The second was that Quibo was but at a small distance from Panama, and we had reason to fear the Spaniards might send a ship of war in search of us, as we had now no hopes that peace had taken place, and had consequently lost all thoughts of surrendering. On these considerations, we plied up to the island of Cano, where we soon did our business, having a good boat. On our passage to that island, the sweetmeats being divided among our messes, one day a man complained that he had got a box of marmalade into which his knife could not penetrate.

On opening it, I found it to contain a cake of virgin silver, moulded on purpose to fill the box, weighing two hundred dollars, and on examining the rest, we found five more of the same kind. These cakes of silver, being very porous, were nearly of the some weight with so much marmalade, and were evidently contrived for the purpose of defrauding the king of Spain of his fifth shares, which he exacts from all silver procured in the mines of Peru. We doubtless left many such cakes behind in the *Conception*, a contrivance that served them both to wrong their king, and to deceive their enemies. A similarly vexatious affair occurred in a prize taken by the *Success*, we heard later, in which there was a considerable quantity of virgin silver in the form of bricks, artfully plastered over with clay, and dried in the sun. Clipperton and his people took these for real bricks, and threw a great number of them overboard as so much rubbish, and did not discover the deception until four or five only remained.

Every thing taken in the *Conception*, was divided according to the articles settled at Juan Fernández, which gave me only six shares, instead of sixty, and the people even refused to allow me the £100 I had laid out of my own money to Hately for supplies at the island of St Catherine's.

I now found myself under many difficulties because the company knew well enough that there was no necessity of going farther than the latitude of 13° N for then steering west to the East Indies. I therefore represented the advantage of cleaning and repairing our ship at Porto Seguro, in California, and at last brought them to my purpose.

9. We sail for California. Description of the Indians, their attachment to us. I think to have found gold.

WE SAILED FROM Cano northwards into gales and bad weather, and therefore ventured out to sea in hopes of meeting more settled weather. When at 180 miles from land the winds still continued variable, but at between 210 and 240 miles, they settled at east-northeast and northeast at which distance we continued till in latitude 20° N. At that distance from shore we were not being sensible of any currents, and were also entirely out of the way of the frightful ripplings and overfalls of water which we used frequently to meet with nearer the land. With these, we would hear the noise of the fall of water as if passing through a bridge a considerable time before it came up to us, after which it would pass us at a very great rate. The ship would only answer the helm wildly; although we could not perceive that we either gained or lost ground, though we sometimes continued in these overfalls for a quarter of an hour.

By getting well out to sea, we were not only clear of these inconveniences, but also out of the way of the vandevals, or seasonable storms, with their hard gusts, black rolling water, frequent and violent thunder and lightning, and heavy showers of rain. In our passage north we were continually accompanied by vast shoals of fish, as dolphins, bonitos, albacores and angel fish. These last are shaped like salmon, and have scales like them, but have tails like dolphins, and nearly resemble them when in the water, appearing in all the beautiful colours displayed by the dolphin. They are the best for eating of any fish that swim near the surface. We were also continually pestered with flocks of the birds called boobies, and their intolerably stinking dung proved an indescribable nuisance, in spite of all the pains that could be taken to clean it off our decks, yards, and tops. We reached the islands of Tres Marias in the beginning of August, but could see no signs of Captain Clipperton having been there. We were also disappointed in our expectation of procuring water, as after the strictest search of all three islands we did not find one spring, though former writers mention their having found water in abundance.

After spending three days in our ineffectual search for water, I thought it best to stand over for the mainland of California, to both procure what was wanting for our ship, and in the hopes of meeting once more with the *Success*. We fell in with the coast of California on 11 August 1721, and as soon as we were discovered by the natives, they made fires on the shore as we sailed past. Towards evening, two of them came off on a bark log, and were with difficulty induced to come on board. Seeing our blacks standing mixed among the whites, they angrily separated them from us, and would hardly suffer them to look at us. They then made signs for us to sit down, after which one of them put himself into strange postures, talking to us with great vehemence, and seeming to be in a transport of ecstasy, running from one to the other of us with great vehemence, continually singing, speaking, and running, till quite out of breath. Night coming on, they were for departing, when we gave them a knife and an old coat each, with which they were much pleased, and invited us by signs to go onshore along with them.

Next morning we sailed, and on Sunday, 13 August 1721, found ourselves near Puerto Seguro, near three white rocks, not unlike the Needles of the Isle of Wight which you must come round to enter the bay. As soon as the natives saw us, some made fires, as if to welcome us, on the tops of hills and rocks near the sea. All seemingly rejoiced to see us; those on shore running up and down to each other, while others launched their bark-logs. No sooner was our anchor down than they came off in crowds, paddling towards us with all their strength, but many more swimming, all the while talking and calling to each other confusedly. In an instant our ship was full of these swarthy gentry, all quite naked. Among the rest was their king or chief, who was no way distinguishable from the rest by any particular ornament, or even by any deference paid to him by his people, his only ensign of sovereignty being a round black stick of hard wood, about two feet and a half long. This being observed by some of our people, they brought him to me, and concluding that I was the chief of the ship, he delivered his black sceptre to me in a handsome manner, which I immediately returned.

Notwithstanding his savage appearance, this man had a good countenance, and there was something dignified in his manner and behaviour. I soon found a way to regale them, by setting before them abundance of our choicest Peruvian conserves, with which they seemed much gratified. They were accommodated with spoons, mostly silver, all of which they very honestly returned, which they would doubtless have done were they gold, the value of these metals being (and perhaps always will be) unknown to Californians.

Having thus commenced friendship with the natives, I sent an officer ashore to view the watering-place and, to make him the more welcome, I sent with him some coarse blue baize and some sugar to distribute among the women. On seeing our boat ready to put off, the king was for accompanying her in his bark-log, but I persuaded him to go in the boat, with which he seemed to be much gratified. The remainder of the day was spent with our wild visitors, who behaved in general very quietly. The officer returned with an account of having been very civilly received, and we prepared our water casks for being sent ashore next morning. Although, at first view, the country and inhabitants might dissuade us from venturing freely among them, I had formerly read such accounts of these people, that I was under no apprehension of being molested in wooding and watering. The Californians, however, appeared very terrible to our negroes, insomuch that one of them, who accompanied the officer on shore, was afraid to stir from the boat and held an axe constantly in his hand, to defend himself in case of being attacked. On the approach of night, all the Indians swam ashore, leaving us a clear ship after the fatigues of the day.

Next morning, at daybreak our boat went ashore with the people appointed to cut wood and fill our water casks, and before the sun was up, our ship was again filled with our former guests, who seemed never satisfied with gazing at us and everything about the ship. That nothing might be wanting to keep up our amity, I sent a large boiler onshore, with a good store of flour and sugar, and a negro cook, who continually boiled hasty pudding, to serve the numerous guests on the beach. At first the natives remained idle spectators of the labours of those of the crew filling the casks but at length, taking compassion at so few men rolling great casks of water over the heavy sand in the sultry heat of the day, they put forth their hands to help them, encouraged by the particular readiness of their chief. For, after seeing Mr Randal take up a log of wood to carry to the boat, he took up another, and was immediately followed by two or three hundred of the natives, so that they eased our men mightily. They also rolled our casks down to the beach, but always expected a white face to assist them, though quite satisfied if he only touched the cask with his finger. This very much shortened the time of our stay at this place. We even found means to make use of those who used to stay all day on board for, when we came to heel the ship to scrape her bottom, we crowded them all over on one side, which, with other shifts, gave her a deep heel, while we cleaned and laid her bottom with pitch and tallow.

The natives seemed every day more and more attached to us. When our boat went ashore in the morning, there was constantly a large retinue in waiting on the beach for our people, and particularly for those whom they guessed to be above the common rank, by their better dress. By this time, the news of our arrival had spread through all the neighbouring parts, and some natives of different tribes from that which dwelt about the bay came daily to visit us. Those who came from any distance in the inland country could not swim, and were differently painted, besides some other visible distinctions, but all united amicably to assist us, and hardly any were idle except the women, who used to sit in circles on the scorching sand, waiting for their shares of what was going forwards, which they received without any quarrelling among themselves about inequality of distribution.

Having completed our business in five days, we prepared for departure on 18 August, and employed that morning in making a large distribution of sugar among the women, and gave a great many knives, old axes, and old iron to the men, being the most valuable presents we could make them. In return, they gave us bows and arrows, deerskin bags, live foxes and squirrels, and the like. That we might impress them with awe of our superior power, we saluted them with five guns on loosing our topsails, which greatly frightened them, and there seemed an universal damp on their spirits on seeing our sails loosed, as sorry for our approaching departure. The women were all in tears when my people were coming off to the ship, and many of the men remained till we were under sail, and then leapt into the sea with sorrowful countenances.

Having made some stay in California, some account of that country and its inhabitants may be expected, though I believe a complete discovery of its extent and boundaries would produce few real advantages, except satisfying the curious. That part of which I saw, the southern extremity of its western coast, appears mountainous, barren, and sandy, much like some parts of Peru, yet the soil about Puerto Seguro, and most likely in the other valleys, is a rich black mould, and when turned up fresh to the sun, appears as if intermingled with gold-dust. We endeavoured to wash and purify some of this, and the more this was done, the more it appeared like gold. In order to be farther satisfied, I brought away some of this earth, but it was afterwards lost in our confusions in China. However this may be, California probably abounds in metals of all sorts, though the natives had no ornaments or utensils of any metal, which is not to be wondered at, as they are perfectly ignorant of all arts.

The country has plenty of wood, but the trees are very small, hardly better than bushes. But woods, which are an ornament to most other countries, serve only to make this appear the more desolate, for locusts swarm here in such numbers that they do not leave a green leaf on the trees. In the day, these destructive insects are continually on the wing in clouds, and are extremely troublesome by flying in one's face. In shape and size they resemble our green grasshoppers, but are of a yellow colour. Immediately after we cast anchor, they came off in such numbers that the sea around the ship was covered with their dead bodies. By their incessant ravages, the whole country round Puerto Seguro was stripped totally naked, notwithstanding the warmth of the climate and the richness of the soil. Believing that the natives are only visited with this plague at this season of the year, I gave them a large quantity of beans, and showed them how they were sown.

The harbour of Puerto Seguro is about two leagues to the northeast of Cape St Lucas, being a good and safe port, and very convenient for privateers when cruising for the Manila ship. The watering place is on the north side of the bay or harbour, being a small river which there flows into the sea, and may easily be known by the appearance of a great quantity of green canes growing in it, which always retain their verdure, not being touched by the locusts as these canes probably contain something noxious to that voracious insect.

The men of this country are tall, straight, and well-set, having large limbs, with coarse black hair, hardly reaching to their shoulders. The women are of much smaller size, having much longer hair than the men, with which some of them almost cover their faces. Some of both sexes have good countenances, but all are much darker-complexioned than any of the other Indians I saw in the South Sea, being a very deep copper colour. The men go quite naked, wearing only a few trifles by way of ornament, such as a band or wreath of red and white silk grass round their heads, adorned on each side with a tuft of hawk's feathers. Others have pieces of mother-of-pearl and small shells fastened among their hair, and tied round their necks, and some had large necklaces of six or seven strings, composed of small red and black berries. Some are scarified all over their bodies; others use paint, some smearing their faces and breasts with black, while others were painted black down to the navel, and from thence to the feet with red. The women wear a thick fringe or petticoat of silk grass, reaching from their middle to their heels, with a deerskin carelessly thrown over their shoulders. Some of the better sort have a cloak of the skin of some large bird, instead of the deerskins.

Though the appearance of the Californians is exceedingly savage, yet, from what I could observe of their behaviour to each other, and their deportment towards us, they seem to possess all imaginable humanity. All the time we were there, constantly among many hundreds of them, there was nothing to be seen but the most agreeable harmony, and most affectionate behaviour to each other. When any of us gave any thing eatable to one person, he always divided it among all who were around him, commonly reserving the smallest share to himself. They seldom walked singly, but mostly in pairs, hand in hand. They seemed of meek and gentle dispositions, having no appearance of cruelty in their countenances or behaviour, yet seemed haughty towards their women. They lead a careless life, having every thing in common, and seemed to desire nothing beyond the necessaries of life, viz., meat and drink, by which means they are free from the anxious troubles to which those nations are subject where luxury and pride have gained a footing. They never once offered to pilfer or steal any of our tools or other utensils, and such was their honesty, that my men having forgotten their axes one day on shore, while cutting wood, which was noticed by one of the natives, he told it to the king, who sent into the wood for the axes, and restored them with much apparent satisfaction. The only thing that disconcerted

them and which they would have mastery over us, was
in our taking snuff, which they would never permit any
of us to use, but immediate on seeing any of us take a
pinch from our boxes, would run up in great earnestness,
take it from our fingers, and throw it away.

Their language is guttural and harsh, and they talk
a great deal, but I could never understand a single word
they spoke. Their dwellings were very mean, being
scarcely sufficient to shelter them. Their diet is, I
believe, mostly fish, which they frequently eat raw, but
they sometimes bake it in the sand. They seldom want
abundance of this food, as the men go out to sea on
their bark-logs, and are very expert harpooners. Their
harpoons are made of hard wood, and with these they
strike the largest albacores, and bring them ashore on
their bark-logs, which they row with double paddles.
This seemed strange to us, who had often experienced
the strength of these fish, for frequently when we had
hold of one of these with very large hooks, made fast to
eight-strand twine, we had to bring the ship to, to bring
them in, and it was then as much as eight or ten men
could do, so that one would expect, when an Indian had
struck one of these fish, from his light float, it would
easily run away with the man and the bark-log, but
they have some sleight in their way of management by
which the strength and struggling of these fish are all
in vain. There are hardly any birds to be seen in this
country except a few pelicans.

When the Californians want to drink, they wade into the river, up to their middles, where they take up the water in their hands, or stoop down and suck it with their mouths. Their time is occupied between hunting, fishing, eating, and sleeping, and having abundant exercise, and rather a spare diet, their lives are ordinarily prolonged to considerable age, many of both sexes appearing to be very old, by their faces being much wrinkled, and their hair very grey. Their bows are about six feet long, with strings made of deer's sinews, but their arrows seemed too long for their bows, and considering that they have no adequate tools, these articles must require much time in making. The shafts of their arrows consist of a hollow cane, for two-thirds of their length, the other third, or head, being of a heavy kind of wood, edged with flint, or sometimes agate, and the edges notched like a saw, with a very sharp point. They made no display of their arms to us, and we seldom saw any in their hands, though they have need of some arms to defend themselves from wild beasts, as I saw some men who had been severely hurt in that way, particularly one old man, who had his thigh almost torn in pieces by a tiger or lion, and, though healed, it was frightfully scarred. The women commonly go into the woods with bows and arrows in search of game, while the men are chiefly occupied in fishing.

I can say nothing respecting their government, except that it did not seem any way strict or rigorous. When the king appeared in public, he was usually attended by many couples, or men walking hand in hand, two and two together. On the first morning of our arrival, he was seen in this manner coming out of a wood, and noticing one of my officers cutting down a tree, whom he judged to be better than ordinary, by having silver lace on his waistcoat, he showed both his authority and civility at the same time, by ordering one of his attendants to take the axe and work in the officer's stead.

One day while we were there, a prodigious flat fish was seen basking in the sun on the surface of the water near the shore, on which twelve Indians swam off and surrounded him. Finding himself disturbed, the fish dived, and they after him, but he escaped from them at this time. He appeared again in about an hour, when sixteen or seventeen Indians swam off and encompassed him and, by continually tormenting him, drove him, insensibly, ashore. On grounding, the force with which he struck the ground with his fins is not to be expressed, neither can I describe the agility with which the Indians strove to dispatch him, lest the surf should set him again afloat. They eventually accomplished this with the help of a dagger lent them by Mr Randal. They then cut him into pieces, which were distributed among all who stood by. This fish, though of the flat kind, was very thick, and had a large hideous mouth, being fourteen or fifteen feet broad, but not quite so much in length.

10. From California to China to England. I have an island named for me. Myself and crew stricken by great sickness. We pass Guam and Formosa but deem it not prudent to put in. We meet Clipperton's crew at Canton and learn of his drunken cowardice in an engagement; one of my men arrested for murder of a customs official. We sail for home in the *Cadogan*, East Indiaman, arriving London, 1 August 1722, after a long, fatiguing voyage around the circumference of the globe of three years, seven months, and eleven days.

ON 18 AUGUST 1721, we set sail from Porto Leguro bound for Canton in China, as a likely place for meeting with some English ships in which we might procure a passage home. Considering the length of the voyage before us, our ship was in a very bad condition, as her sails and rigging were so old and rotten, that if any accident had befallen our masts or sails, we had been reduced to extreme distress and danger, having no change either of sails or ropes, but ours being a case of necessity, we had to run all hazards, and to endeavour by the utmost attention to guard against deficiencies which could not be supplied.

Having already overcome many difficulties, seemingly insurmountable, we were full of hope to get over these also, and the pleasing expectation of revisiting our native shores gave us spirits to try this tedious navigation in so comfortless a condition. We were, in fact, now so weakly manned, that we could scarcely have been able to navigate our vessel without the assistance of the negroes, not amounting now to thirty whites, so much had our crew been reduced by untoward accidents.

We discovered an island on the 21st, 110 leagues west-southwest from Cape St Lucas, but as the wind blew fresh, I could not get nearer than two leagues, and did not think proper to lose time in laying-to in the night. It seemed some twenty miles or so in circumference, having a large bay on its southwest side, in the middle of which was a high rock. My people named this Shelvocke's island. From hence, we shelved down to the latitude of 13° N, but were stopped two or three days by westerly winds, which we did not expect in this sea, especially as being now 1,500 miles from land. The tradewind again returning, we kept in the parallel of 13° N, except when we judged that we were near the shoals of St Bartholomew, and then haled a degree more to the north, and so continued for about two hundred miles.

A fortnight after leaving California, my crew, who had hitherto enjoyed uninterrupted health, began to be afflicted with sickness, particularly their stomachs, owing, doubtless, to the great quantities of sweetmeats they were continually devouring, and also to our common food, chiefly composed of puddings made of coarse flour and sweetmeats, mixed up with seawater, together with jerked beef, most of which was destroyed by ants, cockroaches, and other vermin. We could not afford to boil the kettle once in the whole passage with fresh water, so that the crew became reduced to a very melancholy state both by scurvy and these other distempers. The sickness increased upon us every day, so that we once buried two in one day, the armourer and carpenter's mate. And besides these, the carpenter, gunner, and several others died, together with some of our best blacks, while the greatest part of my remaining people were disabled. To add our misfortunes, our ship now became very leaky, and one of our pumps split and became useless.

Under these unhappy circumstances, we pushed forwards with favourable gales till within 240 miles of Guam, one of the Ladrones, when we encountered foul weather and tempestuous winds, veering round the compass. This was the more frightful, as we were unable to help ourselves, not above six or seven men being able for duty, though necessity obliged even those who were extremely low and weak to assist as they could. In the boisterous seas raised by these gales, our ship so laboured that the knee of her head, and her whole beakhead, became loose, so that the bowsprit fetched away and shook from side to side with every motion of the ship, and so continued all the rest of the time we were at sea. For some time our mainmast stood without port shrouds, till we could unlay our best cable to make more, having knotted and spliced the old shrouds till our labour was in vain. In the midst of these difficulties, I was taken very ill, and had little expectations of living much longer, till the gout, seizing on me, gave me some painful hopes of recovering my life.

In the beginning of October 1721 we made the island of Guam (13° 27' N 144° 47' E). We passed through between Guam and Serpana, and saw several proas, a boat with two hulls, but none came near us that day. We had heavy and squally weather, which obliged me to keep the deck in the rain, by which I caught a cold, which threw me into a worse condition than before, in which I continued all the time I was in China. Guam seemed very green and of moderate height, and the sight of land was so pleasant after our long run, that we would gladly have stopped to procure some refreshments, but durst not venture in, even though some of us were on the point of perishing, lest the inhabitants should take advantage of our weakness.

From Guam I shaped our course for the island of Formosa, to which we had a long and melancholy voyage, as our sickness daily increased, so that, on 3 November 1721, when we got sight of that island, both ship and company were almost entirely worn out. Next day we doubled the south cape of Formosa, passing within a league of the rocks of Vele-Rete, where we were sensible of a very strong current. As we passed in sight, the inhabitants of Formosa made continual fires on the coast, as inviting us to land, but we did not deem it prudent to venture into any of their harbours.

We directed our course from Formosa for the neighbouring coast of China, and found ourselves on 6 November 1721 at the mouth of the river Lema, in twelve fathoms water, but the weather was so hazy that we could not ascertain where we were. Seeing an abundance of fishing boats, we tried every method we could think of to induce some of the fishermen to come on board to pilot us to Macao, but found this impracticable, as we could not understand each other. We were therefore obliged to keep the land close to us, and to anchor every evening. This was a prodigious fatigue to our men, who were so universally ill that we could hardly find any one able to steer the ship. We were bewildered in this mist during four days, and much surprised by seeing a great many islands, omitted in our charts, on some of which we saw large fortifications. This made us believe that the current had carried us beyond our port, and occasioned much dejection of spirits for, though the sea was covered with fishing boats, we could get no one to set us right, or to give us any directions we could understand.

Towards evening of 10 November, as we were passing through a very narrow channel between two islands, a fisherman who had observed by our manner of working the ship that we were afraid to venture through, waved with his cap at us to tell us to heave to until he came to us. When he did so, he seemed to understand that we enquired for Macao, and made signs that he would carry us there, if we gave him as many pieces of silver as he counted little fish from his basket, which amounted to forty. We accordingly counted forty dollars into a hat, and gave them to him, on which he came into our ship, and took her in charge, carrying us through the narrow channel, and bringing us to anchor at sunset.

We weighed next morning, and running close up the coast of China, by noon we were abreast of Pulo Lantoon, whence we could see two English ships under sail, passing the island of Macao on their way from the river of Canton. They kept on their way, taking no notice of us, which struck a damp into our spirits, fearing we should miss a passage for England this season. The afternoon of next day, 11 November, we anchored in the road of Macao, near the entrance of Canton river, which we never should have found by any of our charts. I was much amazed at the incorrectness with which these coasts are laid down to the eastwards of Pulo Lantoon, as there runs a cluster of islands for upwards of sixty miles in that direction, which are not in the least noticed by any of our hydrographers, nor have I ever met with any navigator who knew anything about them. The coast of China, within these islands, is rocky, mountainous, and barren but, owing to my heavy sickness, I was unable to make any useful observations.

As Macao is the place where ships always stop for a
pilot to carry them up the river of Canton, I sent an
officer with my compliments to the governor, and with
orders to bring off a pilot but hearing nothing of him till
next morning, I was under very great apprehensions.
Next morning, the 12th, a great number of the people
belonging to the *Success* came off from Macao to our
ship. I was amazed to see them, and very glad, but my
mind changed a little when they acquainted me that
their commander, Clipperton, had left me by design and
had gone direct to Guam. There he had sold the
governor a great quantity of powder and shot, and other
valuable things, and permitted the Marquis of Villa
Rocha (who was Clipperton's prisoner) to go ashore
with Mr Godfrey, the agent, and a marine officer. As
soon as they were landed, Captain Clipperton weighed
with his ship to attack a vessel from Manila carrying
twenty guns which had been quietly lying in harbour
with them. In approaching this ship, Clipperton ran the
Success on the rocks and soon found the enemy was
prepared for him – for they raised half the ship's guns
to receive him while he was still aground on the rocks.

I am almost ashamed to relate this man's behaviour
in the skirmish that followed, but as I think he serves to
be exposed, I shall relate it as I heard it from his officers,
all of whom talked of it publicly at Canton. Clipperton,
perceiving his case desperate, and the loss of his ship past
redemption, had recourse to a case of brandy to animate

him to making a vigorous defence. But he took so abundantly of the intoxicating cordial that in an instant he became dead drunk, tumbled on the deck and snored out his time in a beastlike manner, while his first lieutenant, Davidson, took command of the ship which he bravely executed until he was killed. He was succeeded by Captain Cook, then their second lieutenant, who as well made a handsome resistance and got the ship afloat again, after she had lain fast forty-eight hours, all which time Clipperton had been lost between sleeping, and drinking as fast as he waked, and sleeping again, and did not recover himself till they were out at sea, and then by his impertinent questions and behaviour convinced all he knew nothing what had passed during their engagement of two days and two nights.

Thus they lost their prisoner the Marquis of Villa Rocha, also Mr Godfrey, and also the marine officer, which gave the ship's company such a distaste of Clipperton that they would not suffer him to have command, and locked him in his cabin, and entreated Captain Cook to take charge of them. They cleared Guam, and had much bad weather in making Amoy in China. There they divided all they had taken, half for the owners, and half for the ship's company. From there Clipperton wished to go for the Malacca, but his people would go no further than Macao, a Christian port. Upon their arrival here Clipperton was arrested by the governor and taken into custody. It seemed while formerly here, he had been arrested for running away with his captain, Dampier's, commission, and also one of his prizes. But this time he could produce his present Majesty's commission for the *Success* so they contented themselves with fleecing him a little. He then sold the *Success* for about one thousand pounds sterling. I have thought it proper to make this digression for such of the gentlemen owners who might have thought him blameless. So now they might pass judgement on his conduct, since it is certain he will never let them into the truth of his story.

About noon this same day, 12 November 1721, a pilot came off to us, when we immediately weighed anchor and entered Canton river, being assured that there still were some European ships at Wampoo, about ten miles short of Canton. We were four days in plying up to the road between the two lower bars, where we anchored and, finding the *Bonita* and *Hastings*, two English India traders, I sent an officer to request their instructions how to conduct ourselves in this port, and to acquaint us with its customs. They answered that the *Cadogan* and *Frances*, two English European ships, were lying at Wampoo; they advised me to send up to the English factors at Canton, to acquaint them with our arrival, and the reasons which obliged us to come here. This I did next day, borrowing one of their flags to hoist in our boat, as otherwise we would have had met with much trouble from the hoppo-men, or custom-house officers.

I sent letters to the captains of the English ships, signifying the necessity which forced me to this country, and requesting their succour and protection, assuring them that I acted under His Majesty's commission, which also I sent for their perusal.

Next morning, being the 17th, I weighed and worked up to Wampoo, where, besides the two English ships, I found three belonging to France, one Ostender, and a small ship from Manila. I now thought to rest a little from my labours, in hopes of all my troubles being at an end, and that I should have leisure for rest and refreshment after my many and great fatigues, expecting to find such treatment from my countrymen as was consistent with humanity and common civility, and with the tender regard and service usually administered to people in distress. But I soon found these expectations ill-grounded, and after all my previous perils, now, proceeding from false brethren, I fell into other, heavier hardships (all circumstances considered) than in all the preceding parts of my voyage.

That evening that we anchored at Wampoo, one of my men, named David Griffith, being in a hurry to remove his effects into the *Bonita* in which he had taken a passage to India, was in the *Bonita's* small boat on his way to the ship when they were chased by a hoppo or custom-house boat which wanted to search them. Being a little in liquor, and fearing they would take his silver, Griffith fired a musket and killed a hoppo-man, or custom-house officer. Early next morning, the dead body was laid at the door of the English factory, where Chinese officers then lay in wait to seize the first Englishman of consequence that should come out. A supercargo belonging to the *Bonita* happened to be the first, and was immediately seized and carried off, and afterwards led in chains about the suburbs of Canton. All that could be said or done by the most considerable Chinese merchants, who were in correspondence with the English, was of no avail. In the meantime, Griffith, who had slain the Chinese officer, together with another man, were both put in irons aboard the *Frances*, which was then chopped, or seized, till the guilty man was delivered up. Griffith was then carried to Canton in chains, and the supercargo was released.

I had not been here many days, when I was deserted by all my officers and men, who, having recovered from their illness, had all now become their own masters and were continually employed in removing their effects from my ship to some of the European ships, without my knowledge, I being then confined to my sick bed. The ship's company had so many ways of disposing of everything they could lay their hands on, that I found it impossible to oblige them to do what I thought of as justice towards our owners. All that were left to look after the ship and to defend my effects, which were on the brink of falling into the bottomless pit of Chinese avarice, were my son and a few blacks.

There were no magistrates for me to appeal to onshore, who would aid me so far as to compel the crew to remain in my ship, and the officers commanding the English ships could not afford me the help they might have been inclined to give, lest the supercargoes might represent their conduct to the East India Company. And these last, who superintend the English trade at this port, seemed even inclined to have refused me a passage in one of their ships, and even treated me as one enemy would treat another in a neutral port, looking on me in that light for presuming to come within the limits of the company, without considering the necessity by which I had been compelled to take that step. For when the captains Hill and Newsham first came visit me, they were astonished at the ruinous condition of my ship, and could scarcely think it possible for her to have made so long a passage from California. The rottenness of her cordage, and the raggedness of her sails, filled them with surprise and pity for my condition. When I had given them a short history of the voyage, and requested they would receive me, my officers and company with their effects, they at once said that they saw plainly my ship was in no condition to be carried any farther, and they were willing to receive us all as soon as we pleased, on payment of our passage. But the supercargoes were displeased that I had not applied to them, as they are the chief men ashore here, though only passengers when aboard, so that I was quite neglected, and the English captains were ordered to take their ships five or six miles down the river below where I lay.

I was thus left destitute in the company of five foreign ships, whose officers, seeing me deserted by my country-men, kindly offered me their services, and assisted me as much as they could, and without them I know not what might have been my fate, as I was under perpetual apprehensions that the Chinese would seize my ship. Soon after, the murder of the custom-house officer seeming to be accommodated by them having the criminal in their possession, a magistrate, called a little mandarin, committed the following outrageous action.

At the beginning of the trouble occasioned by that murder, this mandarin had received warrants to take all the English he should meet, which he neglected to do till all was over. He then one day, while passing the European factories, ordered his attendants to seize on all the English he could see in the shops thereabout, and took hold of nine or ten, French as well as English, whom he carried, with halters about their necks, to the palace of the Chantuck (or viceroy of the province). Application was made to the hoppo, or chief custom man, who represented matters to the Chantuck, in favour of the injured Europeans. On this, the mandarin was sent for, and being unable to vindicate himself was degraded from his post, subjected to the bamboo, a severe punishment, and rendered incapable of acting again as a magistrate, the Europeans being immediately liberated. It appears to me, however, that the English are tyrannised over by the Chinese, and exposed to the caprices of every magistrate, wherefore I was the more urgent to be on board one of the European ships, fearing that I and my effects would fall a sacrifice to their immoderate love of money.

I therefore sent a letter to the supercargoes, demanding a passage for myself, my officers, and ship's company, which I was sensible they could not refuse, but their compliance was clogged with a charge to the captains not to receive anything belonging to us, unless consigned to the India Company warehouse in England. My people being so enraged at this, they vowed they would as soon throw what they had in the sea as comply with such a demand. The hoppo now made a demand upon me for anchorage in the river, amounting to no less than six thousand tahel and, to quicken the payment, annexed a penalty to this extortion of five hundred tahel for every day the payment was delayed. There were no means to avoid this gross and unconscionable imposition, even though I showed him my commission, and had it read in Chinese to him, and though a day necessarily elapsed before I could send up the money, I had to add the penalty of that day, so that he received 6,500 tahel, or £2,166 13s 4d sterling, being about six times as much paid by the *Cadogan*, the largest English ship there, and which was a third larger again than my ship. I soon after sold my ship for 2,000 tahel, or £666 13s 4d sterling, which money was consigned to the India Company, along with all the rest of my effects, and I prevailed on most of my officers and men to take their passage in the English homeward-bound ships.

Considering my short stay in China, and my bad health, I cannot be expected to give any tolerable account of this place from my own observation, and to copy others would be inconsistent with the purpose of this narrative, so that I shall only observe, that the English, at this time, had no settled factory at Canton, being only permitted to hire large houses, called hongs, with convenient warehouses adjoining, for receiving their goods previous to their shipment. For these they pay rent to the proprietors, and either hire the same or others, as they think proper, next time they have occasion for the accommodation.

Notwithstanding my utmost diligence, the business I was engaged in kept me in a continual hurry till the ships were ready to depart, which was in December 1721, at which time, heartily tired of the country, and the ill-usage I had met with, I sailed in the *Cadogan*, Captain John Hall, in company with the *Frances*, Captain Newsham, and as the latter ship sailed much better than the *Cadogan*, she left us immediately after getting out to sea. Finding the *Cadogan* very tender, or crank, heeling too much under sail, Captain Hill put in at Batavia, to get her into better trim.

Here we stayed for about ten days, but I can say little about that place, being all the time unable to stand on my legs, and left her only twice, in a coach, to take the air, two or three miles out of the city, in which little excursion I saw a great variety of beautiful prospects of fine country seats and gardens, and, indeed, everything around showed the greatest industry. As to the city itself, the buildings are generally very handsome, and laid out in very regular streets, having canals running through most of them, with trees planted on each side, so that Batavia may justly be called a fine city, but the sight is the only sense that is gratified here, for the canals smell very offensively when the tide is low, and breed vast swarms of mosquitoes, which are more troublesome here than in any place I was ever in.

A great part of the inhabitants of Batavia are Chinese, who are remarkable for wearing their ancient dress, having their hair rolled up in such a manner that there is little difference in that respect between the men and women. Ever since the revolution in China, which brought that country under the Tartar yoke, the Tartarian dress has been imposed upon the whole kingdom, which was not effected without great bloodshed, for many of the Chinese were so superstitiously attached to their ancient modes, so much so they will unaccountably chose to lose their lives, rather than their hair, as the Tartar fashion is to shave the head, except a long lock on the crown, which they plait in the same manner we do. The Dutch, that politic and wise nation, taking advantage of this superstitious attachment of the Chinese to their hair, and which Chinese live under their protection, exact from all men a poll tax of a dollar a month for the liberty of wearing their hair, which if they charged but a dollar a year, would produce a very considerable revenue, and which, I think, is an unreasonable and unjust taxation upon the Chinese, especially when it is known that the Chinese, so far from being a burden to this great colony, are the chief supporters of it.

Hearing at Batavia that there were several pirates in these seas, Captain Hill joined the Dutch homeward-bound fleet in Bantam Bay, and the Dutch commodore promised to assist Captain Hill in wooding and watering at Mew Island, the water at Batavia being very bad. We fell in with the *Frances*, Captain Newsham, in the Straits of Sunda, though we imagined that ship had been far ahead. Upon us joining Captain Newsham, the Dutch made this a pretence for leaving us before we got the length of Mew Island, and Captain Newsham also deserted us the same evening, so that we were left alone.

We continued six or seven days at Mew Island, during which time several boats came to us from Prince's Island, and brought us turtle, cocoa-nuts, pineapples, and other fruits. Some of the people seeing wild cattle grazing near the beach went ashore to kill some, but before advancing very far saw a small tiger and the track of a large one, on which they retired back to the boat. At this place, some of the gentlemen belonging to the ship, in their outward bound passage saw a rhinoceros.

From Mew Island we had a very pleasant voyage to and about the Cape of Good Hope. By the good ship management of Captain Hill, although the *Frances* and the Dutch ships had seven days start of us, by deserting us in the Straits of Sunda, we yet got to the Cape seven days before the *Frances*, though she sailed considerably better than we. By comparing notes with the officers of the *Frances*, we found that she had suffered a good deal of bad weather off the south of Africa, while we, by keeping about ten leagues nearer shore, continually enjoyed pleasant weather and a fair wind, till we anchored in Table Bay, which we did towards the end of March 1722. Whilst we lay off the Cape of Good Hope nothing remarkable occurred, and this place has been so often described, that I can say nothing of it that has not been said by those who have been here before. We here found Governor Boon and others, bound for England in the London Indiaman. We had a pleasant voyage from the Cape to St Helena, and thence to England, arriving off the Land's End towards the close of July 1722.

Being come into the British Channel, we met brisk gales from the west, with thick foggy weather and on the evening of 30 July we anchored under Dungeness.

That same night some of the supercargoes and passengers, among whom I was one, hired a small vessel to carry us to Dover, where we arrived early next morning. The same day we proceeded for London, and arrived there on 1 August 1722.

Thus ended a long, fatiguing, and unfortunate voyage, of three years, seven months, and eleven days, in which I had sailed considerably more than round the circumference of the globe, and had undergone a great variety of inexpressible troubles and hardships, both by sea and land.

NOTES

1. Shelvocke, George, *A Privateer's A Voyage Round The World* (London: Jonathan Cape, The Travellers' Library, 1930), Preface, p.8.
2. Coxere, Edward, *Adventures by Sea*, edited by E. H. W. Meyerstein, from an original dated sometime between 1685-1694 (Oxford: Oxford University Press, 1945), xxv.
3. Hoffman, Frederick, *A Sailor of King George* (London: John Murray, 1901), p.334.
4. Bushnell, George H, *Sir Richard Grenville* (London: Harrap, 1936), p.68.
5. Betagh, William, *A Voyage Round the World* (London: Combes, Lacy, Clarke, 1728), p.6.
6. Shelvocke, George, *A Voyage Round the World*, with an introduction and notes by W. G. Perrin (London: Cassell, 1928), xiv.
7. Betagh, p.2.
8. Ibid., p.237.
9. Perrin, xix.
10. Sabin, Joseph, *A Dictionary of Books Relating to America, from its Discovery to the Present Time*, Vol II (BiblioLife, Biblio Bazaar, 2008), p.119.
11. Hutchinson, William, *Practical Seamanship* (1777), p.177.
12. Williams, Gomer, *History of the Liverpool Privateers* (London: Heinemann and Liverpool: Howell, 1897), p.403.
13. Ibid., p.37.
14. Ibid., p.4-5.
15. Bushnell, p.30.
16. Innes, Brian, *The Book of Pirates* (London: Bancroft, 1966), p.27.
17. Ibid., p.69.
18. Spate, O. H. K., *Monopolists and Freebooters* (1983), p.383.
19. Perrin, xiv.
20. Betagh, p.23.
21. Ibid., p.20.
22. Ibid., p.34-5.

Notes

23. Perrin, xv.
24. Betagh, p.25.
25. This rank can be taken to mean chief mate according to Clark Russell: 'Rogers's second captain, or chief mate as he would now be called, was Thomas Dover', Clark Russell, W., *William Dampier* (London: Macmillan, 1894), p.140, although Perrin writes 'Hately, the second captain (or 'Lieutenant' as he is described in the High Court declaration)', Perrin, xv. However, as Shelvocke speaks of Matthew Stewart as his 'chief mate', and Mr Brooks as his 'first lieutenant', perhaps Hately was just as described, a 'second captain'.
26. The moidore was a Portuguese gold coin issued between 1640-1732.
27. Betagh, p.25.
28. Quoted in Macintyre, Donald, *The Privateers* (London: Paul Elek, 1975), p.83.
29. Betagh, pp.228-233.
30. Ibid.
31. Ibid.
32. Shelvocke, George, *A Voyage Round the World by the way of the Great South Sea, performed in the years 1719-1722*, edited by George Shelvocke the Younger (London: Senex, 1757).
33. Perrin, xviii.
34. In eighteenth-century Spanish currency, one gold doubloon was equal to eight escudos, or four pistoles, or sixteen pieces of eight. The Spanish milled dollar was a silver coin worth one piece of eight.
35. With a letter of marque commission, a seaman taken prisoner became a prisoner of war with defined rights; with no commission, the taken seaman became a pirate and accordingly could be hanged as a pirate.
36. The Levellers were a radical democratic political action movement which grew out of the breakdown of government and the conflicts of the English Civil War. The name was probably coined by Charles I who referred to them as aiming 'to cast down and level the enclosures of nobility, gentry, and property, to make us all even.'

SEAFARERS' VOICES

A new series of seafaring memoirs

The lives and practices of our seafaring forbears have receded into the distant past, remote but also of fascination to a generation to whom the sea is now an alien place. This new series, *Seafarers' Voices*, presents a set of abridged and highly readable first-hand accounts of maritime voyaging, which describe life at sea from different viewpoints – naval, mercantile, officer and lower deck, men and women – and cover the years 1700 to the 1900s, from the end of the Mediterranean galleys, through the classic age of sail to the coming of the steamship. Published in chronological order, these memoirs unveil the extraordinary and unfamiliar world of our seafaring ancestors and show how they adapted to the ever-demanding and ever-changing world of ships and the sea, both at war and at peace.

The first titles in the series

1. *Galley Slave*, by Jean Marteilhe

2. *A Privateer's Voyage Round the World*,
by Captain George Shelvocke

3. *Slaver Captain*, John Newton

4. *Landsman Hay*, Robert Hay

For more details visit our website
www.seaforthpublishing.com